Turn Off

**A pocket history of Potters Bar
through the eyes of**

John Taylor

**who couldn't find anyone
to write his autobiography**

First Edition Published 2023 by John Taylor

john.taylor2022@outlook.com

56 Mount Grace Road

Potters Bar

EN6 1RB

ISBN 978-1-7393478-1-9

Production - InterPro Publishing Solutions www.interprosolutions.co.uk

This book is dedicated to all those radio announcers who bang on about traffic jams at the junction 24 of the M25 and thus keep the nation aware of the existence of Potters Bar.

Also the lyrics of the Beatles song 'Paperback Writer' which seems appropriate:

"Dear Sir or Madam, will you read my book?

It took me years to write, will you take a look?"

J. T. Spring 2013

PROLOGUE

For a town which hasn't got much going for it and - in truth - never has, gradually its name has become famous for no other reason than the creation of the M25. It has been brought to the notice of the entire nation through the media of radio and TV which frequently mention the place. Potters Bar is now known for traffic jams.

But what of Potters Bar itself? The name isn't particularly romantic or quixotic; it doesn't have the ring of a place which can give you the inspiration to visit it. There is nothing of note or worth a mention - it has no Tourist Centre. As one sage said, it is one of the few towns where there are speed cameras located along the roads leaving the place! It is a turn-off from the M25. Despite that, and against the odds, people seem to tolerate the neighbourhood for all its faults.

It is for this reason alone that I thought of putting together a personal potted history of the time I have spent here so that the frustrated users of the motorway could at least find out about a town that is featured on the news so often. Moreover, I hope that the contents may be of interest to the people that now or in the past have chosen to reside in Potters Bar.

The gestation period of this book has been rather longer than I anticipated and it will become apparent that my skills as a wordsmith will not win literary awards. For that I apologise and seek your indulgence.

So, what does little me remember about that period? Much the same as everyone else who grew up at that time I suspect. There was an austere drabness and greyness about our little world; there was none of the hectic colour that was to become so much a part of the sixties onwards.

So how did this journey start? Well, it goes back to a reunion at my old school in P. B. a few years back ...

Contents

THE SEED OF AN IDEA

'It's been sometime, eh?'

'Sure has. Fifty years. Coo. Seems like only yesterday when I look around the old school'.

'Just think, we used to run around on these very playing fields …'

I was with my colleagues to celebrate the golden anniversary of the opening of Mount Grace school in 1954. Everyone seemed to have aged. Not me, of course, I was still the same.

'Have you come far? We came up from Portsmouth.'

'We're down from Aberdeen'.

'Bumped into someone who had come over from Canada'.

'Manchester, me'.

'Do you remember a chap called Cobb? His family used to run the local baker's shop. He's come all the way from Papua New Guinea with his family!'

'That wimpy chap who was bullied for having ginger hair is here – can't remember his name. He hasn't got any hair at all now, but what he does have is a young stunner on his arm. He introduced her to me as his third wife. He became a pilot, set up a company in America and he said that he had sold it for gazillions.

We absorbed this remarkable fact for a bit and the silence was broken by someone asking me where I lived.

I shuffled my feet a bit. 'Er, not all that far really'.

'Where exactly?'

'Erm. Well, over there', sheepishly pointing to my house overlooking the playing field.

I could sense a lack of expectation: there was a pause.

'Well, I think we all agree there have been huge changes in Potters Bar since we were here. You have lived and witnessed these at first hand - before you turn up your toes you ought to write about it'.

'All those years ago no one had heard of Potters Bar but now it seems to be featured on the radio every other day: 'There is a traffic hold-up near to the Potters Bar turn-off'.

'Well, the town has always been a bit of a turn-off!'

So just like the Velcro man, I was effectively stuck in a sort of a rut of my own choice and felt as sheepish as the bloke who we bullied as a kid. But then I reflected and persuaded myself that I was like fine wine in that it never travels well.

Since I couldn't find anyone who had the slightest interest in writing about me - which came as no great surprise - I resolved to write this modest composition covering my time in the town from the end of the War until the end of the century. I equally resolved that I would be truthful in all things as far as I could remember, even if I had to employ hackneyed phrases for the purpose. Mind you, maybe it's due to sliding towards the selective memory of an old codger's lament.

Whether you decide to grind through or simply dig in and out is, of course, up to you. Either way it is hoped that you enjoy the contents.

IT STARTED NOISILY THEN WENT BARKING MAD

I drew my first breath in November 1942 during an air raid. By all accounts church bells were rung throughout the land which had been requested by the Prime Minister Winston Churchill and readily agreed to by King George VI. This significant act, it seems, may not have had anything to do with my arrival but, I suspect, more to do with the victory at El Alamein at about that time (the last time that the British Army fought alone). The battle was described by Churchill as the beginning of the end of hostilities - although it took another three years to get there. Apparently, the Church of England ditched the rule that women must wear hats in church at the same time.

It would seem that on the same day, my father set foot on Tripoli in North Africa with the First Army. It was three or four years before I was introduced to this strange swarthy man – an experience shared, I suppose, by many children of the same age whose fathers had been away in the Forces.

This notable event - as far as I am concerned - took place in what was known as 'The Kennels' just outside the village of Northaw to the northeast of the town. The establishment was the Greyhound Racing Association where the dogs were housed and trained. The Hook Kennels are covered elsewhere in the book.

My father was a greyhound trainer originally from Yorkshire and my mother was from South Wales. Before they met, she had immigrated to work as an under-house maid - you can't get much lower than that in the service industry - for Viscount Trenchard who lived in Dancers Hill House to the south of Potters Bar. At the time of writing, it is up for sale at £5.25 million. She couldn't have been more than fourteen years of age - an extraordinary fact when compared with the closeted youth of today.

After a distinguished service career in India and South Africa, the future Lord Trenchard was instrumental in forming, during the First World War, what became known later as the RAF. He went on to become Metropolitan Police Commissioner in 1931 followed by other distinguished posts. He was also, I learnt much later, a demanding employer. This haughty man even has two statues, one erected on the Victoria Embankment Gardens and the other at Cranwell Air Force Base. By all accounts he was not a sympathetic employer with an aloofness to the house staff. My mother subsequently went to work for a Mr Tozer, a stockbroker at 'The Grange' in Coopers Lane between Potters Bar and Northaw. It was whilst there that she met my father at a local function where he played the piano.

A little anecdote: I worked for an architectural firm from 1967 at offices in Soho Square, London. Just about the time I was being head-hunted by another firm of architects in January 1971, the partnership decided to relocate to Northaw House! Life had turned full circle - an amazing piece of luck - no more wearisome commuting to London on the tube to and from High Barnet. I decided to stay, but the reasons for moving on hadn't changed really and I eventually left two years later to join Sir Basil Spence and Partners in Tyttenhanger House, London Colney. Whilst at ACP in Northaw there were occasions - it goes with the territory - when representatives of various construction items suppliers and schemes would be called in to discuss their possible involvement and other times when the reps would simply 'cold call'. On one such occasion I received a salesman who turned out to have lived at 'The Grange', being a close relative of the owner. After he left, I reflected, with a little satisfaction I must admit, on how the social tables had been drawn asunder in a generation.

'Hook Kennels' near Northaw village was a strange but wonderful place to grow up in, living effectively 'above the shop'. To live in an area of green fields surrounded by woodland was a magical thing for a young lad. There were other children whose families resided there to join in the adventures. The fields became Wembley in the winter and Lord's in the summer. The woods became an imagined battleground of Cowboys and Indians, Robin Hood and his Merry Men, Ivanhoe, Dick Barton, Cops and Robbers, even trench warfare.

Everyone can remember their favourite Christmas present and mine was undoubtedly a cowboy outfit complete with a Stetson hat, waistcoat with tassels, chaps, a cap gun in a holster and best of all spurs which were later confiscated. My hero was Hopalong Cassidy (for no other reason than my

4

dad was an absolute doppelganger of him). Imagined battles were fought without a clear victory and we took it in turns to be the Red Indians although the latter are now, of course, known as Native Americans.

When we exhausted the gun fights due to the caps running out of our toy pistols, then the adventures morphed into medieval knights rescuing fair maidens, the Crusaders (although we were a bit vague about who they were) battling the Arabs, leading a gang of renegades (again not sure about them either) against no-one, Robin Hood and his Merry Men, Robinson Crusoe and Dick Barton Special Agent. The latter (James Bond had nothing on him!) used to be on the radio and the neighbourhood became suddenly empty as the boys rushed back to listen to his adventures on the radio lasting all of fifteen minutes. I've never forgiven the BBC for replacing him with the Archers.

The radio was and still is important to me. Plays especially - the pictures that are created in one's mind are much better than theatre, moving pictures or television! This lifelong pleasure was started by a 'crystal set': a coil, a crystal and war issue headphones fixed to a piece of wood. No electricity was necessary. In order to pick up the radio waves it was necessary to dangle a piece of wire which acted as an antenna/aerial from the set via the window to a tree in the garden. I was told in no uncertain terms that in the event of the threat of a thunderstorm it should be taken down in case it attracted lightning and burnt down the house. The chances of that happening are a few trillion to one I should think, but I still removed it if there was a threat of rain!

We had no television then – it was simply too expensive and it seemed by general consensus that it was pretty rubbish and would never catch on. A black and white screen nine inches square in a huge box showed a blurred picture that was forever going wrong. There was a daily programme on one BBC channel for an hour in the afternoon and two hours in the evening.

When we did eventually install a TV (on hire purchase, I imagine, or more likely rented) it was a very sedate affair. People on the screen were very polite to each other and to us the viewers. They dressed nicely and spoke nicely. They had names like Sylvia Peters, McDonald Hobley and Peter Dimmock. The gentlemen had neat haircuts and, I'm sure, clean shoes and the ladies were dressed in formal frocks. If anything went wrong, they blushed bright scarlet or more accurately bright grey. Away from the joys of Sylvia who, I once overheard from one of the grown-ups was quite a dish (what's food got to do with it?) and the embarrassing Muffin the Mule and the Flowerpot Men, ours was a simple world. I suppose we had a vague awareness that there were a few people somewhere out there who had pots of money, but Mum and Dad seemed to have enough for our needs and there was none of the contemporary wall-to-wall parading of other people's wealth, lifestyles, and cars, along with attractive partners, that creates such a sense of misguided frustration and jealousy in so many people today.

Sundays were different. We were not allowed to wear dungarees or play ball games, for some obscure religious reason I suppose. Washed and brushed up, we were sent to Sunday school at Thomas a Becket church in Northaw village up a long 'bumpy' Hook Road. We were given coloured stickers to go in a book depicting pictures of Jesus carrying out miracles presumably to prove we had attended and not skived off. If we had attended every lesson, we were given a gift. The only one I remember was a toy mincer. I wasn't quite sure what I was supposed to do with it and in the absence of any meat, put earth into the top, turned the handle and not surprisingly, broke it. I waited for a miracle repair in vain.

I was christened at the church when I was a baby but of course my dad was fighting the Germans at the time, so he wasn't there. However representatives of the four services (Army, Navy, RAF and the Marines) were apparently present at the time - although it's sad to report that two of them didn't survive the war. One of them was my mother's brother Brin, who was killed in Nijmegen in Holland as part of what became known as 'A Bridge Too Far'. He was nineteen. His name is on the cenotaph in Potters Bar High Street (B. E. Thomas).

I had an extended family since my mother persuaded her family to leave the misery of the Rhondda coalfields to join her in Potters Bar before the war. Thus, her father, who had been a miner, and her mother came over with their three younger children – two brothers and a sister moving into a two-up-two down rented house at 93 Southgate Road (with an outside toilet). Not a great location as it turned out, for a V2 rocket launched from Louisianan Site 19 in Holland had landed nearby at 11.16 am on cold and icy Saturday morning on 20 January 1945 - with just 107 days of war remaining. Twenty-nine civilians were killed (5 died in hospital) and 34 more seriously injured, with 72 slightly injured. The Catholic Church was severely damaged and half a dozen houses were flattened, with other buildings having their roofs blown off and windows blown out. A millisecond either way they wouldn't have survived. As a result of the bombing 40 buildings were destroyed or damaged beyond repair. A further 3,032 buildings were damaged but capable of being repaired out of 4,100 in the whole district. For those now living in a pre-war houses in the town now, there is a 74% chance that it was repaired.

So why was Potters Bar the target from these devastating war heads? There was no strategic reasoning what with a modest population and no manufacturing or armament factories. It wasn't until after the war when information filtered through that double agents were informing the enemy that their rockets of mass destruction were landing on heavily populated areas of London along with factories, munitions, communication centres and so on, whereas they were diverted to less densely occupied locations and Potters Bar happened to draw the short straw and cop one of the dreaded V2s.

HOOK KENNELS

Hook Kennels no longer exists, but either side of the War it was a hive of activity with a large workforce serving several stadiums in London. Amongst them were Stamford Bridge, Catford, Walthamstow, Harringay, Stamford Bridge along with White City. Sadly, the latter no longer exists. It was the main venue of the 1908 Olympics and held over 68,000 seats. At the time of writing there are only two left, namely Wimbledon and Catford, and these are struggling. The whole dog racing scene - often described as a working man's horse racing – is no longer as popular as it was due to other forms of entertainment and the introduction of easier means of betting along with pressure from the animal rights lobby.

Exercising the Dogs

The oval tracks and mechanical hare were introduced to Britain in 1926 by the American Charles Munn, in association with Major Lyne-Dixson, a key figure in coursing. Finding other supporters proved to be rather difficult however and with the General Strike of 1926 looming, the two men scoured the country in an attempt to find others who would join them. Eventually they met Brigadier-General Critchley who in turn introduced them to Sir William Gentle. Between them they raised £22,000 (equivalent to £1.7 million in 2022) and launched the GRA. On 24 July 1926, in front of 1,700 spectators, the first greyhound race took place at Belle Vue Stadium where seven (later six) greyhounds raced round an oval circuit in order to catch an artificial electric hare. This marked the first ever modern greyhound race in Great Britain.

The kennels were purpose-built to serve most of the London stadiums and were sited within grounds of approximately 70 acres, most being parkland which was divided into paddocks for each trainer to exercise and train (the greyhounds not the staff!). There were quadrangle blocks, mostly consisting of 25 kennels. Each had a concrete floor together with a raised bed 12 inches above the floor containing straw.

There were eight trainers who lived in the semi-detached cottages situated in Hook Lane (they are still there, now privately owned. I was born at number 2, with the rest of the staff either living locally or billeted in accommodation on site.

Hook House

Hook House was built largely from materials of nearby Gobions, Brookmans Park, in 1839 featuring low pitched roofs. Inside there is an excellent 17th century staircase from Gobions.

Brigadier-General Critchley lived in the big white house which is now the Oshwal Centre (see end of the chapter). It was run, I imagine, very much like an army camp. The other management included Colonel Cameron and other 'officer' class men including Mr Bateman the veterinary surgeon. The trainers were sort of non-commissioned officers, the head lads corporals and the rest 'other ranks'.

Transporting the dogs from the Hook Kennels was quite an undertaking.

Huge yellow vehicles looking a bit like removal lorries containing individual kennels were a common site which used to trundle through Potters Bar to evening meetings twice a week in the late afternoon on the way to the various dog tracks in London. With the crowded roads nowadays, it would be a logistic nightmare. They also took the same journey at other times for trials. What this meant is that the dogs were timed so that they would be allocated into races against other dogs of similar speed – a sort of handicap - the theory being that they would all end up in a straight line at the finishing post. The bookies and the Tote kept a close eye on these times to work out the odds at the start of the races.

Each trainer was responsible for about thirty plus dogs and bitches sharing

the same kennel though not when the latter were 'in season'). They were exercised twice a day in paddocks, seven days a week, so lots of walking usually six at a time; it took a lot of skill and patience to stop the leads becoming entwined. The trainer's role was to make sure they were up to scratch to race. Prior to this, puppies were taught to accelerate out of the starting boxes and keep going until the end of the race. Decisions were made on the best distances and whether they were suitable for hurdle races. Contrary to what some people think, greyhounds are generally pretty docile. In order to keep them in shape the diet was mainly cereal with little or no meat, which meant that along with the grooming each dog received on most days, a toothbrush was also used to protect their teeth!

On Sunday mornings the owners of the dogs would often turn up and it was the trainer's duty to be there. After petting their respective mutts, they would then furtively enquire whether there was any 'stable information' on possible winners at the next meeting. If the tips came off, then perhaps a bit of 'dropsy' would hopefully come forth. Employees of the GRA were not allowed to bet but I'm sure they found a way round it. What this all meant was that I saw little of my father – it was a full-time job with knobs on.

The fact is that if you look after animals, you can't take a day off no matter how terrible you feel. He absolutely had to get up and get going every day. His photo on the *left* is at White City with the betting tote reels behind.

In 1942 'The Hook' became an Army War Dogs Training School. By all accounts the greyhounds 'left' at the behest of the War Office. Where they went, I have no idea although I fear the worse. A specialist unit of army trainers along with administration and ancillary staff moved in. There were about eighty dogs of various breeds under the control of the War Office (MT2) which carried on until the end of the war.

Quite a lot of the people who worked there came from areas of the country which suffered in the recession of the thirties. Economic migrants - to use the modern vernacular - except, of course, they came from within the UK rather than from overseas. A case in point is my father who came down from Yorkshire and my mother from South Wales. An extraordinary piece of luck as far as my existence is concerned which led, I suppose to my contrary - at times – personality, with the bluntness of a Tyke and the sentimentality of the Welsh. Still, as they say, opposites attract.

Trainer Taylor with Dogs

Whereas greyhound racing was hugely popular either side of the Second World War with thousands of punters piling into the various stadiums throughout the country, its attraction slowly waned from the late fifties onwards. Competition from TV, Bingo halls and so on had an effect. But the main reason was the introduction of betting shops. Until then it was only possible to bet at the track or via a telephone account. Bookmakers would sometimes set up a base in a friendly pub, hire 'runners' to tell what the odds were at that time, collect bets, and pay the winners, while lookouts warned about policemen. The bets were small, but the excitement was high. The Police were reluctant to enforce the law or may, God forbid, have taken a pay-off for looking the other way. The working-class communities strongly supported the bookmakers who were providing entertainment and employment. The Betting and Gaming Act of 1960 finally legalized off-course betting. Turnover increased by 154% in the next year, with over 13,000 licences for betting shops in operation. What this meant is that it was no longer necessary to 'Go to the Dogs' to bet and in consequence attendance inevitably faded away.

It is worth reminding ourselves that in the early 20th century the parliamentary Labour Party vigorously opposed off-track betting on horses using bookmakers. Middle class reformers were trying to shield the working class from the evil and harmful effects of gambling, Some Labour MPs laughed at this approach, but after 1920, with the rise of union influence in the Labour Party, the position changed to one of relative toleration and acceptance, using the slogan, "*There Ought not to be One Law for the Rich and Another for the Poor which is the Case Today.*" The laws were deliberately fashioned to control and restrict the working classes, and now they had a political vehicle to object. Middle-class reformers were outraged, and the working class delighted, with the emergence in the mid 1920s of a new entertaining sport and betting. Greyhound racing fitted the bill - it seemed modern, glamorous, and American, although the middle class lost interest when a working-class audience took over. The greyhound racing industry peaked in 1946 with attendances estimated to be around 75 million and tote betting of £196,431,430 at that time. The figure equates to £9.4 billion today (2022). Audiences started to decline with the opening of betting shops in 1961.

The writing was on the wall and as a consequence of greyhound tracks closing in London, the Hook Kennels sadly closed for ever. The site was taken over by developers and dwellings replaced the kennels and outbuildings although the original trainers' cottages remained. 'The Hook House' and a large proportion of the remainder of the estate – in the area where the paddocks were located - was taken over by the Oshwal Association (Jain community) in 1980.

Oshwal Centre

The temple was built in 2004-5 consisting of pink sandstone, with an interior of white marble, quarried and carved in India before being shipped to England. In the precinct are several other structures including 24 shrines. Well worth a visit.

FOOD GLORIOUS FOOD

The period after the war was austere in many ways and the cost of basic food as a proportion of the weekly budget was much higher than today. The country's finances were disastrously poor, flirting with bankruptcy, at the end of WW2, and as we had turned more than 55% of our economy to armament production, the UK had to perform a painful readjustment in order to return to a peacetime economy.

This was not helped by the USA suddenly terminating Lend-Lease in 1945. The UK had been relying on Lend-Lease imports of food and just could not afford to pay for imports due to lack of exports (by 1945, exports were barely at one-third of the level that they had been in 1939). The USA had provided a loan of $4.33bn (equivalent to US$78 billion in 2022) that was supposed to tide us over until we got back on our feet. British politicians had been hoping for a gift, but the USA was not that generous.

Unfortunately, one of the US loan conditions was that we made sterling convertible. Within a month, nations with sterling balances had drawn almost a billion dollars ($145m in 2022 dollars) from our dollar reserves and we had to devalue, making imports even more expensive. And now we had to use our scarce dollars to pay the loan back. Bear in mind this salient fact when politicians talk about the 'special relationship' of our oldest ally. Yeah, right... *It's the economy stupid' - a phrase that was later coined by James Carville in 1992*. Friends across the pond? Forget it!

To add insult to injury, many of our foreign currency-generating assets had been sold at fire-sale prices early in the war to pay for US arms shipments (Cash and Carry was replaced with Lend-Lease when Britain was within months of going bankrupt in 1941) and many of our foreign markets had been irretrievably lost. A salutary fact is that the last payment on the US loan was made in 2006. So quite simply Great Britain could not afford to buy food from abroad, resulting in rationing of basic foodstuffs which did not end until almost ten years after the war. Growing vegetables in the garden or allotment was a necessity and not a pastime as it is now. We kept chickens in the garden at Northaw and if they stopped laying eggs their necks were rung and after plucking and drawing (ergh!) we had the rare luxury of roast chicken for Sunday lunch.

The expenditure on basic foodstuffs as a proportion of average income in the fifties was hefty when compared to modern times and certainly the variety we now take as granted from the supermarket could only have been dreamt of during those austere times.

Even recycling scraps of food happened but in a most odd way. Pig bins used to be put out on some verges every so often and people used to dispose of waste food such as potato peelings into them for collection although strict instruction was given not to put in rhubarb leaves as this apparently didn't go down well in the stye.

It is a salutary fact that in 1957 food took up a third of the family budget whereas now it is about 8% in 201 (excluding alcohol). Food has become cheaper, partly because of supermarket price wars, huge container ships and planes importing food, often frozen, easily from throughout the world. The big minus is that this encourages wasteful habits: according to 'WRAP' the average home now wastes a quarter of a tonne of food a year, the equivalent of 50 meals. Half the waste results from food not being eaten before its 'use by' date and most of the rest is from cooking or serving too much. Bring back the 'Pig Bins' I say.

There were no 'sell by' dates on products – it was simply a matter of little tasting or the use of your nose. Plastic packing was non-existent products were just put in brown paper bags or not at all. Vegetables from the greengrocer were simply shovelled into your bag or basket after bei weighed. The same was done with nuts at Christmas although the cunning retailer used to pour water over then to make them weigh heavier!

As far as us kids were concerned 5 February 1953 was a wonderful day as this was when sweet rationing ended. Along with other children all over Britain we emptied our piggy-banks and headed straight for the nearest sweet shop. By all accounts toffee apples were the biggest sellers, with sticks of nougat and liquorice strips also disappearing fast. Up until then the maximum allowance was 1lb per month – half a bag of sugar.

THE HIGH STREET AFTER THE WAR AND WHAT HAPPENED DOWN THE HILL

Potters Bar High Street was and continues to be a busy bustling thoroughfare. Originally it was the main A1 route to and from London and the north. It was known as the 'The Great North Road' and essentially followed the original Roman route. Then in 1928 the 'Barnet By-pass' was constructed and transferred the increasing traffic. The road through Potters Bar then became the A1000 and the new road eventually became the A1(M).

After the war the High Street consisted of shops and retailers to cater for seemingly everything (rationing excepted of course) - very different from now. There were four pubs where only one survives now: One of them The Green Man still exists as a listed building I'm glad to say, fronting new housing. It was rumoured and assured by those in the know but never proved that this is where Mr Potter, who was the landlord at the time, put his bar, or entrance to the toll road, across the road and this is how the town got its name. Also, the highwayman Dick Turpin hid there on his way from London to York on Black Bess or at the very least jumped over the tollgate. All fanciful, I fear. Further up was the Robin Hood, then the White Horse (now the Cask and Stillage) and at the crossroads The Lion – now a sort of café. This pub is a listed building apparently, one of the few in the town although you wouldn't think so given the garish signage and strings of lights that spoil the appearance. Hertsmere planners and Councillors don't seem to care - but more of them later!

Traversing south and starting from the police station - now a nursery school - there was the 'Men's Institution' subsequently taken over by the British Legion, now much reduced to cater for the site development into flats. Previously it was the 'Village Hall'. The bus garage had a beautifully tended lawn in the front now sadly concreted over as a car park for the staff. Opposite was a parade of shops which still exists. From memory there was a hat shop/milliners, a motorcycle repair shop, Hooneys the greengrocer, a grocery store, a café (which my parents briefly owned and ran some years later) and the Victoria wine store. The grocery store was owned by the A1 dairies which ran a fleet of milk floats from the rear.

I don't remember all the shops opposite to where the war memorial was moved to from a fork in the road to the north, other than it had the only eating establishment in town that opened in the evenings; unlike now where there are seemingly dozens of both sit-down and take-away eating places which have expanded exponentially. There were no 'take-aways', that's if you don't count the fish and chip shop which only opened during the day and never on Mondays.

Salisbury House opposite The Walk, then owned by the Council but flogged off, is still there (more of this later). Here were meeting rooms for Council business along with a doctor's surgery on the ground floor and a dentist on the first. The surgery moved some years later and is now in the Walk and the dentist followed to a converted house almost opposite.

Next door on the east side the first parade of shops consisted of an establishment that sold - ahem - ladies' undergarments, called, I think, Ritas. Then Walsh, a men's outfitters, followed by a sweet shop then Tolmers the butchers, further along a wet fishmonger. Payment was made to most of the larger food shops not to the staff who served you but to a lady who sat in a kiosk at the back. The price/amount was written on the wrapping paper. To this day I have never understood why the staff couldn't add up or maybe they weren't to be trusted...

There were a couple of barbers above the shops. The most alarming thing that ever happened to me as a kid was that on one occasion the barber produced a lighted taper and singed my hair! It was apparently fairly common in those days although the theory behind it leaves me quite cold (unlike my scalp at the time).

Further along was the Co-operative store, the only outlet still in existence but much different today. After purchasing the goods and having the coupons cut out of the Ration Book, a note was made of your membership number – in our case 493474 – and we were given tin coins which I suppose were collected to claim the 'Divi' at some stage in the future. Again, this was done at a kiosk at the back of the shop. Opposite was the Westminster Bank – now a nursery – along with Cobb's the Bakers where you could buy warm ha'penny rolls, and Brays the newsagents. Next to Ladbroke School was a house that had chickens in the front garden. Further along was an Estate Agents called Whiteson and Pill - a most peculiar title conjuring up in my infant mind a man in white with his little son holding a pill.

Then there was a garage owned by the elderly Burgoyne twins with petrol pumps that swung out into the road, later replaced with a standard forecourt. To my young eyes it was a big building for car repairs and at the back there was a disused blacksmiths forge presumably for the use of a farrier since the High Street was once well used by stagecoaches. Just as well the hot coals weren't in use at one end with petrol at the other. Almost opposite was Barker's the hardware store owned by the jolly owner Jim (the second generation of the family business) who had twin boys who took it over until it closed in 1987 - there must be something in the water in that neck of the woods that produces twins. I was engaged to design the building it replaced.

Next door was the Robin Hood Hotel with assembly rooms although I don't think there was accommodation available. I believe it was called 'The Robin Hood and Little John' originally. It had a flat roof which replaced the previous pitched roof which was blown off and never replaced because of the V2 rocket that landed in Southgate Road (see page 6).

Further along was Boots the Chemist with its lending library on the first floor. I was given a membership card for a Christmas present and I'm ashamed to admit that I still have a book I borrowed entitled 'Conjuring for Boys' which I failed to take back when it closed. I've still got it in anticipation of when they decide to open a library again.

There followed another greengrocers, Clements, and Sainsbury's with its long line of marble counter tops on either side. No self-service then: the customers said what they wanted and the shop assistants would set out the order on the counter. There were chairs for the elderly or weary shoppers to sit on in front of these counters. Butter was taken off a big slab and the assistant would skilfully 'butter pat' it on to greaseproof paper to the quantity requested. Equally the cheese was pared away from a huge lump by means of a wire cutter on a wooden board. Bacon was sliced on a mechanical contraption to whatever thickness was requested. It seemed a lot of work to me but perhaps it was to do with the rationing at that time. Again, payment was made at a kiosk at the back of the shop. There was also 'Williams Brothers' and 'International Stores' although I don't remember any exotic foodstuffs from foreign climes on display; however, they did deliver - not by a van but by delivery boys on bicycles adapted with a huge basket in front. My uncle Brin, who was killed in the war, was one such assistant after he left school at 14. Thus, four relatively large food outlets - for the time - to choose from, all competing against one another one assumes.

Barclays Bank was located further up (now an eating establishment with garish signage). In front of the pub car park was a small shop selling sports goods, owned by Harry Collins who went on to teach handicraft at Mount Grace School. I used to knock around with his daughter Josie. Next to the pub was Twyman's garage, another doctor's surgery - Dr Mary Allen - followed by Cobb's the Chandlers which sold animal feed and flour scooped out of a sack. Then there was Weston's the drapers and haberdashers (who had a sister shop at the north end of the High Street) ending with the Greyhound Garage that swept round into Southgate Road.

Opposite was a tobacconist - Hunts. The shop front was full of smoking paraphernalia: pipes, snuff and cigarettes, with small dishes of loose tobacco with little signs saying 'Best Shag'. Could there have been a hidden supply of 'Worst Shag' inside for those smokers who were short of money? There were shelves of cigarette packets - some with cards inside to collect and stick in albums. Cheap cigarettes such as Woodbines and Park Drive could even be bought in packets of five. Affordable for the young lads (no age restriction to buy) who had been encouraged to take up the weed by sweet cigarettes and pipes made of liquorish when they were younger. Alongside was a men's and boy's outfitters - Hodgkinson's - who sold and had a cartel on school uniforms which could not be bought anywhere else.

There were a couple of other shops which sold cigarettes along with sweets which were sold loose from huge glass jars, weighed out on a scale and shovelled into a bag . Amongst them were gob stoppers (good value as they lasted a long time) which changed colour as they got smaller, sherbet dips and pear drops but rarely chocolate which wasn't good value because of the cost (and the fact you had to cough up the sweet ration coupons).

At the end (where the 'Favourite Chicken and Ribs' is now) there was a Chinese laundry. Along a bit further and opposite the White Horse was Tingey's - a huge (at least in my youthful mind) two storey furniture shop set back with a wide pavement in front.

My elder sister mentioned that she recalled Kleenall cleaners, another greengrocer and 'Powers Electric' shop and Harris the cobbler along with two cottages and a large shed to the right of Tingey's.

Continuing south past the traffic lights in Barnet Road on the east side was the Post Office (now an Indian restaurant), Burnett's sweet shop (run later by my uncle and aunt) and further down a milk depot (now Magnet) followed by Page Calnan, a builder's merchant which is still there but now owned by Travis Perkins. On the other side opposite the post office was a funeral parlour (now a garage repair shop) then an empty space and a beautiful garden where there is a car park now, and finally the garage which is still there – although in those days the petrol pumps fronted the road and the cars to be filled up with petrol were parked at the kerb side with the hoses extending over the pavement so people could walk underneath.

So, there you have it. From what I can remember: four pubs, five grocers, four garages, four greengrocers, a wet fish shop, five tobacconists/sweet shops, two butchers, two banks, two bakers, a fishmonger (one I think) along with seemingly every other retail outlet that might be needed from haberdashery to cobblers. Oh, and two cafes and one evening restaurant. As mentioned earlier, never in my wildest dreams did I think that all these years later there would be so many eating establishments - at the beginning of 2023 there were 63 to cater for the hungry masses!

There were no supermarkets. You went to different shops for different items. For fruit and vegetables, you went to the greengrocer. For meat, to the butcher. For fish, to the fishmonger. For bread and cakes, to the baker. For groceries such as jam, tea, biscuits and cheese you went to the grocer. Other shops sold clothes, shoes, medicines, newspapers and all the other things people needed to buy. There were no cars to take the purchases home. Shopping was carried out pretty much every day in consequence.

Refrigerators after the war were not very common. Perishable goods were stored in a larder with a marble top to keep the perishables cool and a little opening with a fly screen. It is interesting to note that up until the sixties it was still a requirement under the Building Regulations for these to be compulsory in every dwelling despite most houses having a 'fridge' by then.

The most radical difference to retailing today was the hours of opening: Monday to Saturday usually 9am to 5.30pm with a half-day closing on Thursday. Banks closed at 3pm on weekdays. No popping down to the all-day grocers 'Open all hours' - hard luck if you forgot something earlier. Pubs were usually open 11am to 2.30pm then 5.30 to 10.30pm. Even these hours were reduced on Sundays.

As well as all the retail outlets in the High Street and to mitigate against having to struggle home with the shopping, a veritable army of home deliveries were in full swing. Milk was delivered every day and other traders such as bakers, laundry and even soft drink companies were a common sight. There were still some horse-drawn delivery vehicles. Coal, of course, was the main source of heating and was delivered via sacks to most houses since gas central heating was a commodity found only in expensive houses.

But what it did mean was that along with rationing this led to a healthy diet. Children were given free vitamin C in the form of orange juice along with Cod Liver Oil in addition to free milk at school. Sweets were rationed. It has been argued that 'War babies' were the healthiest there have ever been before or since in the UK. We didn't go hungry at home although some meals were boosted by 'fillers' such as bread and butter, along with the luxury of tinned peaches after meat and two veg for Sunday lunch.

I don't remember many overweight kids in those days compared with the modern generation (latest statistics show that one in 3 children in the London area are overweight). In 2021/22 research showed that in every thousand 10 & 11 year olds in England 234 were obese and 143 overweight. There weren't many fatties around, when I was a kid, that's for sure.

Another factor may be that most homes didn't have central heating so to maintain body temperature, converting food into heat depended on how much the body temperature exceeded the surrounding temperature. Nowadays, of course, heated buildings mean that that this temperature difference is reduced and thus less energy is required.

The end frame in comics would often reflect this: Desperate Dan in 'The Dandy' would be sitting in front of cow pie or Korky the Cat in 'The Beano' tucking into a fish as a reward after their respective adventures.

Unlike today, Potters Bar High Street was the main shopping centre: this has been largely moved to Darkes Lane. Tesco's and Sainsbury's have muscled in. I can't think of any other town in England of comparable size that has two 'High Streets' but I am prepared to be corrected.

Development over the years created retail outlets that challenged the High Street, so much so that eventually Sainsbury's and Boots relocated along with banks and other shops to Darkes Lane. A modest hotel had been built by the station followed by a cinema before the War. As a result of this a ribbon of shops along with the Council Offices was developed and consequently the town spread westward; simply put, a town split into two. After a while Herts County Council, which had taken over from Middlesex in the early seventies, urged a demise of the High Street as a main retail hub in favour of Darkes Lane by refusing a supermarket opposite the bus garage. Ironic, as a few years later Tesco breezed in and created its present supermarket next to the High Street without a peep from County Hall. Draw your own conclusions. More on Tesco's later.

Darkes Lane developed unhindered and even boasted Woolworths (now Superdrug), the nearest the town would ever get to a 'department store'. Electricity and gas showrooms arrived, a main Post Office and retailers pretty much mirroring and eventually overtaking the High Street to a certain extent. Of the shops, a particular one of note was Samson's where you could buy all sorts of ironmongery and tools. It was a treasure trove run by an intense little man who could seemingly satisfy every mechanical demand. If you wanted a nut and bolt of a certain size, he could find it - even down to the type of screw thread. I'm pretty sure that if you asked for barbed razor wire or goods to manufacture a bomb, he would find them stashed away. Then one day a small grocer's shop arrived called 'Payantake' which was quite innovative at the time being a self-service arrangement imported from the US. It caught Tesco's greedy eye before long and it took it over.

As a young lad I worked one summer holiday as a shelf stacker and gofer from 8am to 6pm for 4 shillings (20p) per hour. The premises were crammed and the store at the back stacked so high that it was almost impenetrable. Even the outside yard had boxes with tarpaulins over them with mouse traps underneath! One day a little bad-tempered bald man with a big nose arrived unannounced and strutted around grumbling at everyone for not working hard enough. He complained to the manager that he was not made of money and that he was using too many small paper bags. I later learned that this tyrant was the owner, Jack Cohen.

Now Tesco's supermarkets are ubiquitous throughout the nation; their net worth as of January 2022 was £30.43 Billion. The moral of the story? Look after the small paper bags and the billions will look after themselves.

Tesco's in the fullness of time would have a huge effect on the town as a whole. It became its nemesis. The company pulled down our cinema and replaced it. Not satisfied, it then pulled down our hospital and did the same.

ong with Sainsbury's they then slowly strangled the small retail outlets:

EXAMPLES OF POTTERS BAR RETAIL OUTLETS IN THE LATE SIXTIES:

From 'The Official Guide to Potters Bar' by The British Publishing Co. Ltd 1969

12 butchers	7 D.I.Y & Household Merchants
7 Chemists	8 Ladies Fashions
2 Coal Merchants	7 Ladies' and Childrens wear
6 Drapers	5 Laundries
6 Fishmongers	7 Newsagents & Stationers
4 Florists	7 Off-Licenses
1 Furrier	2 Pet Stores
10 Greengrocers	6 Post Offices
13 Grocers/General Stores	6 Radio & T.V. Sales & Services
4 Hardware & Ironmongery	16 Tobacconists & Confectioners
9 Public Houses	8 Toy Shops
3 Gent's Outfitters	9 Wool Shops

Not forgetting 8 Pubs (in the town & nearby)

Potters Bar is, of course, not alone to witness the demise of the shopping experience. Supermarket and online purchasing have taken its toll, but even so it is a pity that the variety and competition has died on the vine. Still, we've got lots of fast-food outlets, estate agents, hairdressers and charity shops so that's all right then…

HEALTH AND SAFETY

Health:

There weren't many books at home other than a huge Holy Bible (although religion wasn't a big factor in the family, it must be said), Pears Soap Cyclopedia and a large medical book: in the event of not feeling very well, the latter proved to be the go-to reference to find out what was wrong. Leafing through the contents, it appeared that the symptoms you were suffering from were more serious than you first thought so that a slight chill was clearly the start, amongst other things, of swamp fever at the very least or perhaps beriberi. I have no doubt on reflection that a whole plethora of these diagnosis books must have been on sale before the creation of the National Health Service and the notion of self-analysis. National newspapers before the creation of the NHS would often have huge advertisements on the front page for medicine such as Andrews Liver Salts. Not - ahem - 'The Times' of course!

Parents made their own contribution towards keeping their children fit and healthy by dosing them with cod liver oil and *Haliborange* tablets which looked like mini rugby balls. Some boys would suffer from boils on the back of their necks for no apparent reason. Occasionally we were given thick, brown, sticky gloop called *Virol* for reasons which weren't quite clear. A home remedy for removing wax in the ears was to pour peroxide into the cavity which would bubble away - how on earth we didn't go deaf in consequence is a mystery. One of the biggest fears was poliomyelitis (polio) and after the vaccine was developed in 1952 by Jonas Salk from the University of Pittsburgh, the entire population of children in the 1950s was immunised.

School children of the fifties could expect to be off school sick at least once a term - and whilst at school, this new generation of National Health Service kids could expect to be poked and prodded by a phalanx of doctors, nurses and dentists keeping a watchful eye on their health. The latter was an awful experience when at regular intervals children were dragged to the dental surgery in Cranborne when teeth were yanked out under 'gas' and chucked into a wicker basket (the teeth not the kids). Fillings were shoved into cavities created by a drill worked slowly on a treadle connected via a long arm of rods with a cable loop. Unlike modern high-speed drills, the dentist would grind away whilst pumping with his foot in the hope that the 'cocaine' would last long enough. Still, it must have kept them fit I suppose even if the patient felt equally exhausted.

Regarding the medical treatment, Potters Bar Hospital was built on the site of what is now Tesco's and was transferred from its original location in Richmond Road. It was paid for by public subscription and taken over with the formation of the NHS. It was a relatively modern building for one floor designed to facilitate additional storeys at a later date. There was uproar or at any rate great unease from the folks of the town and huge regret that the site was sold. It went for £1.5 million – not a bad deal for the supermarket I would suggest. A condition was that the supermarket would cough up and build a much smaller replacement which is now in Barnet Road on the site of a building called 'Howgate' effectively for Community Care rather than Secondary Care which the original hospital catered for. A clever deal for the retailer but not for the general public of Potters Bar that's for sure. The new facility was smaller by some measure with inadequate parking.

At about eight years of age, I found myself in the hospital to have my tonsils removed which was a common occurrence for most kids in those days. It was an awful, harrowing experience. With no pre-op, I was wheeled into the operating theatre where a muscular nurse pinned my arms to the side whilst a rubber gas mask was plonked over my mouth and nose. It was a dreadful suffocating, traumatic and distressing experience which resulted in nightmares of drowning afterwards. Three years later I found myself in the same hospital to have polyps removed from my nose and I was so scared I ran away the morning before being admitted.

Safety:

- Baby cots were covered with brightly coloured lead-based paint, which we chewed and licked. We had no childproof lids on medicine bottles, childproof latches on cabinets and, come to think of it, childproof anything.

- We drank water from shared bottles and I can't remember anyone becoming ill afterwards.

- We would spend hours building trolleys out of scraps nicked from a dangerous junkyard and sped down hills; only to find out that we had forgotten to install brakes. After running into garden walls and stinging nettles a few times, we learned to solve the problem by wearing out the soles of our shoes. Or do something else.

- We played football, rounders or cricket that went on for hours or until it became too dark. We were responsible for our own safety.

- We walked to school and pretty much everywhere else. If it was too far to walk and when we were old enough, we rode a bicycle without a helmet or caught a bus or a train - often on our own. We didn't rely on Mum or Dad - even if a car was available. It was a treat to ride in the passenger seat without seat belts or air bags.

- We made up games and ate stuff that might have been alive. Although we were told it was bound to happen, the live stuff didn't carry on living inside us forever and I can't remember anyone losing an eye.

- We fell out of trees, cut ourselves, broke bones and teeth. We had fights, punched and pinched each other without any adults interfering and if we didn't like it, we kept out of the way.

- There were no lawsuits since our actions were our own. Consequences were expected. The idea of a parent bailing us out if we broke a law was unheard of - they usually sided with the law anyway.

Boys' games were in their own way somewhat disorganised and in modern eyes could be considered almost brutal. One example was 'British Bulldog': for those who don't know the rules, a string of boys would line up and face a single opponent standing stoically alone. The purpose was to get past him. Easy enough, you would have thought, except the perambulation was carried out by hopping on one leg with the arms crossed. He would charge into the opponents and if he was successful in making them put their redundant leg on to the ground (or crash to the floor) they were effectively captured and thus added to his team. As the game went on, his increasing army would line up against the diminishing opposition until there was but one left. This singleton would then take over the role and the whole affair would start all over again. Bruised and battered with scorched knees, like mini-soldiers returning to the trenches we would limp our way home at its inevitable conclusion.

But this was nothing when compared to 'Hi Jimmy Knacker' which needed a convenient wall in order to play. Two sides were selected alternately by various means. The fattest boy of one team would lean with his back against the wall with his legs apart to act as a cushion. The next boy would bend down and put his head between them. This was followed by another who would put his head between the second boy's legs as in a rugby scrum. The rest of the team would do likewise so that a snake was formed. So far so good.

The other team would then line up and leapfrog on to the opposition's backs in an attempt to make it collapse. If it did the whole narrative started again. On the other hand, if the snake managed to stay solid after the entire team had piled on top, the roles were reversed, but only after the battle cry of 'Hi Jimmy Knacker 1-2-3' had been yelled in unison - if somewhat muffled - after prompting from the cushion man. All this took place without adult supervision for if there had been, even in those unenlightened days, the game would surely have been banned.

Unlike these days of equality, girls were separated from rough boys' games. If anyone suggested at that time the female species would play football, rugby and cricket at international level no-one would have believed them!

Our generation has witnessed an explosion of innovation and new ideas. We have experienced freedom, failure, success and responsibility, and we learned how to deal with it all. And all this before lawyers and government regulated our lives for our own good. It's amazing we've survived.

SHORT-TROUSERED EDUCATION PART1

Every day my mother would walk with me in school term time along with my baby brother in a pram to and from Northaw to Southgate Road - a return distance of perhaps 3 miles a day. My elder sister used to cycle. It's difficult to believe now, when present-day kids are transported everywhere, including to and from school. The reason for this was that my elder sister attended Parkfield Secondary School located in The Walk opposite the Cricket Club since there wasn't a secondary school in Northaw. I was dragged along and attended St John's Infant School at the top of Southgate Road.

It was difficult for me since I was no longer with my friends at home who went to the local school in Northaw and I didn't know anyone in Potters Bar. It didn't help at lunch time for when everyone else was tucking in and running around afterwards in the playground I went to my grandmother's house for 'dinner'. So, there I was - at a school where I didn't have much opportunity of mixing with the other children in the same way as the friends in Hook Lane. On reflection, as a consequence of this, I inevitably found myself alone most of the time with little social skills to interact with my contemporaries at school although in truth I wasn't entirely uncomfortable in the world in which I found myself caught between two stools. I became, in effect, a bit of a nonentity. A skinny shy kid with a xylophone torso. Difficult to imagine now but I developed a stutter.

Whilst on the subject of Southgate Road during the war - a little anecdote. My mother's sister either lived with or was staying at my grandparents' house when a long snake of an Army convoy trundled down the Great North Road through the High Street from a supply camp somewhere up North and turned left on the way to the London docks or more likely

Harwich. Her husband was one of the red caps and the lorry in which he was travelling conveniently and coincidentally broke down outside their very house. Whilst the lorry was being fixed, my uncle - I subsequently discovered - took the opportunity of popping inside to claim conjugal rights whilst the lorry was being 'fixed'.

But back to St John's School. It was named after the church in the High Street which no longer exists and was located where the cenotaph is now situated. The school was built as a result of the 1870 Forster's Education Act and opened in August 1872. It provided virtually free elementary education for anyone who wanted it, but the truth is that the industrial revolution needed workers who were able to read and write as well as do basic arithmetic. There was pressure from industry for literate recruits. Education for children up to the age of ten years was made compulsory in 1880 and it was only after this time that the streets were effectively cleared of ragged children living on their wits. The site was eventually levelled in 1964 and flats were built on it eight years later.

The design and layout of the school was pretty much replicated throughout the country and was based on the ideas of E R Robson who was the first architect of the London School Board and adopted the 'Queen Anne' style of architecture which was partly a reaction to the Gothic Revival at that time. The building that contained Ladbroke Junior School in the High Street (and still stands and is fortunately a protected building see page 41) was somewhat similar. Both educational establishments were somewhat forbidding and institutional with windows high enough to prevent children looking outside and being distracted, unlike the acres of glass surrounding later schools.

So, there I was in a Victorian educational establishment. Originally it had just one large classroom. After a while this proved to be inadequate and pretty impossible for the poor teachers (who were paid by results) covering a wide age range. It was extended to provide school dinners (which were cooked off site and transported in) along with two wooden huts constructed at the rear.

All desks had lids and were in rows facing the front. There were specific lined exercise books for practising letter shapes. When we were older we had ink in little inkwells, and horrid scratchy nibs making ink splatters.

I am indebted to Elizabeth Light (nee Fysh) who was in the same class as me, for her memories of that time: **'I guess I must have started there in 1948 when I was already five. I am not sure what the admission criteria were then. Today children go at the beginning of the school year in which they become five. Why is it that school dinners figure so largely in the memory? The dinner tables seated eight children, four each side on a form or bench. The hall gradually cleared as those children who ate their dinners were sent out to play. Lunches were pretty grim after all, but it was the bowl of gloopy tapioca with a spoonful of jam in the middle that I just would not eat.'**

Teaching was much more formal than nowadays with the desks in regimental formation in front of the teacher who was behind a huge table on a raised dais. One teacher I vaguely remember was a Mrs (Miss?) Mills. She was a large straight-laced stern lady whose upper torso was redolent of a roll-top desk. To keep some semblance of control she said that when she turned to write on the blackboard, she had eyes in the back of her head - which we all believed of course - although how they could see through the severe bun was a bit of a mystery. Another was Miss Parish (the boys called her Miss Parachute). I've an idea that her boyfriend, or less likely her husband, used to meet her after school and they walked into the sunset hand in hand. Could have been juicier come to think of it, but as you know sex didn't exist before 1963 according to Philip Larkin.

There was a lot of chanting in order to learn things by rote, particularly times tables. You simply HAD TO GET IT RIGHT - it worked though. There wasn't much 'play' in the classroom although rather oddly both girls and boys were taught sewing and needlework. For some reason the correct order of the alphabet was important; we were taught in tranches and even to this day – and as an old man – I have engraved in my mind's eye A - F being on one line and G being the start of the next and so on. Most odd. The Jesuit maxim 'Give me a child until he is seven and I will give you the man' does come to mind.

There did seem to be a lot of 'accidents' (not me though!) where nervous pupils were either afraid or embarrassed to be excused. The caretaker always had a bucket of wood shavings handy for such an eventuality. The lavatories were outside at the end of the playground without a roof; in the case of the boys, it contained pungent smelling urinals along with WC

39

booths without doors. I don't know how the adjacent girls' accommodation or the aromas come to that compared. All the boys wore short trousers – winter and summer – held up by braces and they had to ask the teacher to undo them at the back when they were caught short, much to their embarrassment. No wonder the wood shavings were in demand.

All the kids walked to school, of course, usually in wellingtons even when it wasn't raining. We all had a slipper bag hung on individual pegs and these boots were exchanged for the plimsolls inside when we arrived. My grandmother, who was a seamstress, made a lot of these on her treadle Singer sewing machine. I don't know how much she charged but it couldn't have been very much.

At this time the country was slowly getting itself back together after the War and although the town wasn't affected as much as other places - other than the V2 rocket mentioned earlier - there was some evidence around. Rebuilding and repairing of most of the houses in Southgate Road and the High Street took place and prefabs were speedily built in Gregory Avenue. I recall some years later climbing all over a crashed burnt-out fighter aircraft, pretty much near where the Oakmere Library is now, which hadn't been cleared away some years after it had crashed.

SHORT-TROUSERED UNDER EDUCATION
PART 2

In the early fifties we moved from the tied cottage in Northaw to a house in Tempest Avenue which coincided with the start of my junior education at Ladbroke School. A welcome change to a school nearby and no more wearisome trudging cross country through all weathers! Similar to St John's infant school, the original building fronting the High Street reflected the nationwide design criteria of that time. The practical implications of having all these children in one big room presented almost impossible problems I have no doubt. Ventilation, heating, lighting as well as acceptable sanitation must have caused almost daily difficulties when catering for often grubby children. The fact is the educational overlords who emerged at the end of the nineteenth century were essentially a conservative body on the question of school design and layout and were not keen, partly to do with the shortage of teachers, to adopt separate classrooms. The overriding element in all this was inevitable - cost. The old poor law tradition of providing minimal accommodation at the lowest price was manifest and the School Board was anxious to avoid allegations of extravagance.

When I arrived at the school it had been extended from the single original Victorian building (which was converted into a kitchen) to four classrooms and assembly hall which still exists. Due to the increase in the town's population and the raising of the school age, wooden HORSA huts were subsequently added. St Mary's Church Hall was also used and for those of us who were billeted there it was the nearest we would experience to how it must have been to attend a public school with its high ceilings and ecclesiastical feel. Further HORSA huts were erected in Parkfield School which were also used at times.

At the other end of the town, Cranbourne School was built at about the same time as the extension to Ladbrook. There are now seven primary schools (including Little Heath) dotted around the town with both Ladbroke and Cranbourne being rebuilt and relocated near to the original sites. A secondary school at Parkfield (to cater for the whole town) was built and opened on 23 September 1938 which was later demolished to make way for retirement accommodation with the playing fields taken over by Potters Bar Town Football Club along with the new Ladbroke School. There were also two notable private schools in the town. Lochinver and Stormont for boys and girls respectively. The former wore pink jacket and caps which proved to be the equivalent of red rags to a bull if we spied them.

So, when I arrived fresh-faced and bushy-tailed complete with a school cap the next stage of my education began. My first teacher was a Mr Tharpe think that was his name). The only thing that sticks in my mind is being taught 'joined-up writing'. I recall he very carefully copied from a book on to the blackboard what the letters should look like - presumably on strict instructions from the LEA. This baffled me - fancy being taught by a teacher who couldn't write! The following year my class teacher was Mr Barker followed by Mr Reavley. It was very different to the present time where male teachers, at primary school level, are an exception. Thus, all through primary school I was taught by men. This is very unusual nowadays which was confirmed in an article published by 'The Times' recently which opened by saying that boys are shunning degrees because female teachers are dominating schools and 'feminising' education. The chief executive the Universities and Colleges Admission Service stated that convincing evidence of gender imbalance generated problems with some boys.

At the time of writing there were 455,000 teachers at state schools in England: 74% of them are female, as are 91% of teaching assistants. It could be argued that this must have a detrimental effect on boys especially those who are being raised by single mothers. The most disturbing fact is that only two higher educational institutions have a specific target to recruit more male students. As the report concludes, 'This is a serious problem'.

Once more I am indebted to Liz who reminisces: *'Dinners and playground games were what stick in the memory. The playground games went in seasons. In high summer it would be mainly handstands against the brick wall along the outside toilets. In winter the playgrounds were never cleared of snow. The boys made slides, black, glossy and treacherous. Our final year was spent in a Pratten hut at the Secondary school, Parkfield. You could be hit on the hand in front of the class for misbehaviour and I hated Miss James for it. Once a week the whole school filed into the hall for 'community singing'.'*

My memories were a little different, mainly because boys and girls were strictly segregated most of the time like alien beings. Free milk appeared each morning break time and being given the heavy responsibility of milk monitor was a first taste of power. A straw was issued to each of us. We never had straws at home, so this was quite unique although I was once reprimanded for bending mine and when I asked for another, I was told in no uncertain terms that there was only one each per week.

At playtime it was time to use our imaginations and invent games with rules so complex we'd forgotten them the next day. Teams would form and disband, bonded together with magic passwords. Gangs of boys used to march around cajoling others to join in whatever games were decided to set one gang against another. 'Join in for Cowboys and Indians' was the most popular. By the time it was organised there was little time left before the whistle went to herald the end of the break. An exception occurred in 1950 when a general election took place when 'Join in for Labour or Conservatives' took over. The Tory supporters - posher kids - outnumbered the Labour lot which I naturally joined. Unlike the parliament socialists who squeaked in with a narrow majority, we lost the ensuing battles through sheer weight of numbers.

More reminiscences from Jeremy Bonnett: *'Lunches were provided in aluminium containers via a lorry from Cranbourne School at St John's and the smell permeated throughout the classrooms - it stank and I would refuse to eat it - particularly the ubiquitous cabbage! I remember Misses Jones and James, both Welsh and probably very young but they seemed quite old to me. Then we moved to Parkfield and scratchybum Mr. Reavely. I struggled with work and duly failed the dreaded Eleven Plus.'*

No ball games were allowed unless you count marbles: a coloured glass orb was flicked into a roughly drawn circle and if it hit an opponent's marble outside the circle, you added it to your collection. Girls did a lot of skipping accompanied by chanting whilst jumping in and out of the rotating rope. If it rained, hard luck - you just put on a raincoat - and if it was freezing cold the boys made slides to keep warm. We were fiercely territorial about them, and the right to go on a particular slide had everything to do with your place in the pecking order of friends or foes. I was once banned when after close inspection the others decided that the scratches on the surface were a result of the metal 'Blakey' protectors on the heels of my shoes.

In fairness, there were more organised school team games later such as football for the boys. I am not sure what organised games the girls played (as mentioned previously we were segregated!). I was fortunate to make the school team to play other schools. We were dished out rather faded musty pre-war jerseys with a string collar. Boots were heavy leather affairs - mine were second-hand - in which studs were hammered into the soles (I still possess a metal last for some obscure reason) and coated in much dubbin to make them softer and a bit of waterproofing which never worked as promised on the tin. Unless you were fortunate to be taken to watch professional teams, no-one had much of an idea how to play. There was no football on the television other than the Cup Final once a year.

Just like St John's, the boys' and girls' toilets were separate from the main building in the opposite corners of the playground. We were trooped in before dinner to wash our hands with great lumps of carbolic soap but rather oddly it was kept out of bounds when we used the outside toilets. Dinner time in the hall was ruled assiduously and irrespective of what was put in front of you, it was compulsory to eat it all up. Grisly meat usually followed by semolina pudding with a splurge of jam was quite awful - but it still had to be eaten since we were reminded how lucky we were when compared with the starving children in China ('Well, they wouldn't like to eat this!'). I was once given a severe rap on the hand with a ruler by the headmistress for having the temerity to suggest that I was more than happy to send the food on to one of these starving children, wherever China was.

Thus, presumably all over the country at school dinnertimes, mashed potato was dolloped out by grim dinner ladies wielding ice cream scoops - and a torrent of lumpy custard was ladled over a million roly-poly puddings. There was no choice - and there was always fish on Fridays. 'Drink up your milk and eat your greens, all of them' was the mantra in a world just emerging from wartime rationing, which still existed.

Talking in class was strictly forbidden. Anyone caught was made to stand in the corner or sent outside the classroom door until the teacher was satisfied that the culprit had learned his or her lesson. It is difficult to realise now that corporal punishment was something we expected if we didn't do as we were told. It was a whack with the cane, or a ruler on the hand. Cracks across the head were not uncommon for lesser misdemeanours. Such discipline was supposed to guarantee respect for the teachers. Whatever happened, you didn't go home and tell your parents because they would as likely back up the teachers and at the very least continue the chastising.

In my final year the whole school was transferred to the secondary school at Parkfield which had been vacated by moving to the new school at Mount Grace. St John's School mentioned earlier took our place. I was pushed up a class (don't ask!) with Mr. Reavley which meant I had to make new friends which I found difficult and I was absent quite a bit pleading some sort of imagined malady.

There was community singing on Friday afternoons - sitting cross-legged in the hall and bawling out soppy songs. If you had a straight back and it was noticed, you were allowed to leave five minutes early. In the fourth year everyone went to a freezing, grubby swimming pool next to a restaurant called San Marina in South Mymms on a Friday afternoon. Other than splashing around in the sea on a beach, I had never learnt to swim. I feared water and made all sorts of excuses to get out of the lessons. This was after the first time when, decked out in knitted swimming trunks which absorbed water like a sponge, reducing buoyancy, I found it impossible to float let alone swim. Worse still, it shrunk my willy to almost nothing…

Two days were set aside in the early spring for the dreaded Eleven Plus examination which determined whether you went to Grammar school or not. I don't recall being prepared for this by the class teacher. I was chastised for some misdemeanour the second morning and was given the cane - not the greatest preparation for a very important event! It came as no great surprise to find out I had failed along with most of my fellow candidates.

There is often a lot of debate and handwringing about SAT tests, but believe me, it was nothing compared to the Eleven Plus. The latter was geared to IQ (Intelligence Quotient). None of us had had any experience of the type of questions found in the examination papers. These tests were used – as it says on the tin – to determine 'intelligence' and their efficacy has now been argued by learned educationalists and others to be questionable to say the least. Subjecting immature youngsters to a seminal hurdle which would have an effect on the rest of their lives is cruel and I am astonished that there are still parts of the country that trumpet and defend the return of such demarcation.

At that time – the early fifties - seismic changes were taking place in the town which affected education. Since there was an urgent need for housing to replace the vast war-damaged buildings in London, the authorities at the time put together suburban areas to take the overspill, and given the relatively close proximity and ease of transport, Potters Bar was an obvious target. Housing estates were planned to cater for this influx of people, predominantly from Tottenham and Edmonton. As a consequence it was necessary to build a larger secondary school to cater for the subsequent increased numbers of children. A brand-new modern school was planned - not 'Secondary Modern' like Parkfield - but Comprehensive, clearly a step up in the educational stakes, although most of the local population didn't twig what its philosophy alluded to. The post-war Labour government was anxious to widen the 1944 Education Act and question its intrinsic fault-line based on the notion to determine children's future (and the rest of their lives) on the strength of a one-off Eleven Plus examination of questionable validity.

Since Potters Bar at that time was in the County of Middlesex and there was no 'grammar school' as such, then it followed that a new education establishment to reflect this mantel was created.

So, by an astonishing piece of luck I had the opportunity of attending a brand-new educational establishment within walking distance - what was there not to like?

The alternative? It is worth mentioning that those few pupils who passed the Eleven Plus faced tortuous bus journeys within Middlesex. There was no cross-pollination between the LEAs. Nearby schools which were in Hertfordshire, such as Barnet's Queen Elizabeth Boys and Girls Schools were simply unattainable. This strict demarcation and allocation resulted in the ridiculous situation of, for example, children living in Little Heath (a stone's throw from Mount Grace School) in Hertfordshire having to catch a bus to and from Barnet whilst children in, for example, Finchley travelled in the opposite direction. The two nearest grammar schools that most went to - Minchenden and Southgate County - were a long bus ride and walk taking over an hour each way. The Local Education Authorities (LEAs) simply didn't talk to one another, secure in their own fiefdom. Barmy.

Whilst all this was going on, it is worth mentioning that most reading matter, films and TV programmes at that time only ever included public schools. From Billy Bunter to Enid Blyton's Famous Five and Secret Seven and from Tom Browns Schooldays to Greyfriars's, the schools depicted were simply alien environments to most children. It wasn't until Grange Hill arrived on TV in 1978 that most youngsters could identify with their own educational experiences, even if those experiences might have shocked their parents.

IN THE RIGHT PLACE AT THE RIGHT TIME

By sheer luck as far as my generation in the town was concerned, a brand-new comprehensive school which became known as Mount Grace and generally regarded as being well-designed and set in delightful surroundings, was created in the town. It was officially opened a few weeks after I arrived in 1954.

The school's inspired and innovative layout was visited by both home and overseas architects and engineers, which led to a RIBA medal being awarded. This later resulted in the Consortium of Local Authorities' Special Programme (CLASP) being created which led to the template for hundreds of both primary and secondary schools along with further education buildings throughout the UK. Thus, Potters Bar can be justly proud that Mount Grace was not only original in this field, but a vanguard of innovative and sound design. A combination of prefabricated curtain walling with occasional traditional brick walls created a pioneering template with standard components fitted to a steel framework radically reducing construction costs and the period of construction. Admittedly the said curtain walling had alarmingly high thermal conductivity but at that time fuel (initially coal which was later replaced by oil then finally gas) was relatively cheap. Very different from nowadays.

Original Parkfield School in the Walk

49

The design and rationale of the school layout was quite different from the one it replaced at Parkfield which was effectively a monolithic block, containing all the classrooms and administration hubs around a courtyard to let in light. This reflected Le Corbusier philosophy of open area between buildings and to make worthy use of external space in its surroundings. Undoubtedly, this created a pleasant environment. But it did have the disadvantages of long runs of services and access. Distances between blocks worked fine until it rained. The covered ways only worked when the rain fell vertically which rarely happens!

The big advantage of the school site realised at the design stage is the south-facing slope of the land which flattened, ideal for physical exercise and games. The education blocks were arranged to take advantage of this southerly aspect. The overlooking of greenery and mature trees were carefully retained and the school publicity photographs often showed this off. In the same way, the classrooms in H block and the canteen overlooked the Rose Garden. The hard-standing main playground is well hidden from view and isn't really overlooked because the hall windows are set high. A special mention should be made of the hall, which was without doubt quite splendid, flooded in natural light. It has a stage that would be the envy of many professional theatrical companies although changes to the entrance mean it has been spoiled.

As an illustration of inflation, I understand that the whole of the school, including furniture, was less than £750,000 pounds nowadays, significantly less than a typical detached house in Mount Grace Road opposite.

Mount Grace School was superbly designed in delightful surroundings. Potters Bar can be justly proud that through Middlesex County Council, Mount Grace was not only original in its field but a vanguard of good design although it should be pointed out that there was - and is an alarmingly high thermal conductivity to the external envelope, but then again the building was built with boilers using relatively cheap coal.

The big advantage of the school site realised at the design stage is the south facing slope which flattens out which was ideal for physical exercise and games. The education blocks were arranged to take advantage of the southerly aspect with the end of the entrance drive left free to open up the vista on to the oasis of the 'Headmaster's Lawn' and over the girls gym, no longer there but I shall get to that later. The overlooking of greenery and mature trees by the classrooms in L block and A block created a most pleasant vista with the access corridors located on the north elevations. It was an inspiration to retain the original rose garden in front of the house and that is why the school entrance was located further east. A special mention should be made of the hall which without doubt is quite splendid: it has an extraordinary roof span and is flooded with natural light. It has a stage that would be the envy of many a professional theatrical company.

Over the years it is inevitable that school buildings are altered to reflect social and educational changes. No more bike sheds (where do the lads go now for a furtive fag?) or regimented single sex cloakrooms, and the introduction of computers, self-catering and so on. But the essence of the design and elevations of the school have been guarded and retained. All that philosophy came crashing down when it was decided to replace the girls' gymnasium with a Sports Hall. It is criminal therefore that an overpowering monolithic Sports Hall has replaced a perfectly good girls'

gymnasium facing the playing field which has had to be compromised. This was despite objections not only to the non-standard footprint over the accepted matrix for full and wide use of various sports, but also to the Lego- inspired architecture which made no effort to fit in with the rest of the school buildings. It now appears much as Prince Charles once said about the extension to the National Gallery - as a monstrous carbuncle on the face of a much-loved and elegant friend.

Before and after photos below

I found out at the 'public meeting' that the school (the end user after all) had no say in the project whatsoever - the Department of Education was paying for it, so it took over the brief, engaged a contractor ahead of the architects who came up with an appalling box which ended up two metres higher than the approved drawings. When I pointed this out to the Hertsmere Council Enforcement Officer, he said that it was 'marginal'. Try that if you want to build another storey on your house! I have designed numerous sports halls and recreational buildings since the seventies and the process always followed the accepted avenue: brief from the end user, client approval, planning approval and then go out to tender, with penalties if running over time on site. All these factors were totally ignored by the DoE.

Just to add insult to injury, at the time of writing the project is still not finished and has been on site longer than it took to build the 80 storey Empire State Building, New York, in 1931. It offends my eye whenever I look out of my bathroom window...

WILLINGLY TO SCHOOL

The seminal time for everyone who lives in the UK is undoubtedly moving into secondary education. By sheer luck as far as my generation were concerned, a brand-new school under the title of Comprehensive – one of the first of its kind – was planned and built such that I arrived just before its official opening on 30th. October 1954.

So, there I was, resplendent, like most of my contemporaries, in a green blazer which was far too big for me ('You'll grow into it'), and short trousers. Oh, and the cap. I was confused and a little scared: it's not so bad nowadays, when children are quite rightly given a taste of school life before the big day. Despite the rationale of comprehensive 'child-centred learning' the six entry forms were segregated according to perceived learning abilities based presumably on the aforementioned eleven plus.

We were herded into the playground, blinking at the seemingly huge buildings surrounding us, waiting to be allocated to a classroom became a form room where we were issued with a dip-in ink pen, a pencil, eraser and hymn book which were to last the entire time at the school. We were streamed and I found myself in the second tier - I have no idea how or why. I didn't know anyone really - most of my contemporaries at junior school had either passed the Eleven Plus, moved to private education or else were in the top stream. The form teacher was a Mr Cresswell who had arrived at the school at the same time and seemed to be equally intimidated and unsure. I discovered much later he had a distinguished war record in the RAF.

The setup was completely different from junior school where the class teacher did everything from English to P.E. and all the other subjects in between. Here it was different. Different teachers for different subjects in different locations - some were better than others. If you talk to retired teachers, they say that in general they can't remember most of their former pupils other than those that cause problems. That is equally true from the other perspective. In my case it was the French teacher, a Mrs Stevenson. She looked a bit like the Queen Mother or Grannie in the Giles cartoons with a desk-top bosom. She waxed continually about her wonderful son and when she spoke in French, well, it didn't sound French.

One day, a girl in our class brought in a French pen pal, and when Mrs Stevenson tried to converse with her, she kept saying *'Je ne comprends pas'*. Such was this grounding in a foreign language, it was no surprise that my linguistic skills were doomed from the start.

The staff in general at that time, at least for the first years, had a pot pourri of teaching skills. Most had had a grounding in secondary modern education and seemingly either ignored the rationale or struggled with the unknown comprehensive system aiming towards examinations and further full-time education. A proportion of male teachers had been fast-tracked via training courses after the War (it was only nine years since the Armistice, after all). An example was one Jimmy Golding who had gone into teaching after a career as a PTI in the RAF. He taught me mathematics in the first year, then French the following year, although he seemed more comfortable on the parade ground – rather than the playground!

The four houses created and made by Caroline Swash (nee Payne)

In fairness, there were some members of staff who had degrees in their subjects, but there were in the minority at that time. The headmaster was an enthusiastic advocate of comprehensive ideology but nonetheless took on board the ethos of grammar schools - he was particularly keen on the House system (Romans, Saxons, Normans, Danes).

He swanned around in a gown and every morning made a grand entrance from the back of the hall for morning assembly but was rarely seen in the classroom. In the background there were a number of parents and others who seemingly aligned themselves to a quasi-Fabian Society trumpeting this, as they saw it, the foundation of an egalitarian society. As mentioned earlier the school was staffed by teachers who had cut their teeth in structured secondary modern education; a proportion were fast-tracked as general teachers from the war services. The huge rise in the birth rate - now known as 'baby boomers' - meant that the standard was compromised. In fairness it was a mammoth task to take on the role of teaching a wide range of pupils' abilities. The consequence was that the classes were streamed, with little movement occurring, which was rather against the idea of 'comprehensive'.

During the post-war period the country had to build up its manufacturing base once more and in order to compete with the rest of the world turned its energy to manufacturing, it was considered essential that a workforce should be provided to reflect this. Accordingly, great play was made on the practical skills needed, at least as far as boys were concerned, and an entire day of the week was spent in the workshops. Strangely this didn't include the girls. They did domestic science and needlework, presumably in preparation for motherhood, and later shorthand and typing in readiness for office work. Looking back, this was an extraordinary division of subjects according to gender. This curriculum was, naturally, at the expense of other more, shall we say, academic subjects, putting some pupils such as myself at a distinct disadvantage to other young people being educated in grammar schools (not to mention in public schools) and the subsequent roads to further full-time education.

Whilst I was busily playing conkers and Hi-Jimmy-Knacker with my mates, without my knowledge a maelstrom of debate raged throughout the land on secondary education as a result of the Education Act of 1944. Grammar, Secondary Modern, Technical and now Comprehensive. This is best described in the book 'Modernity Britain 1957-69' by David Kynaston and published by Bloomsbury.

Weeks went by in the first year and we slowly found our feet, although in my case I had to go into hospital for an operation and was out of circulation for several weeks. No attempt was made to help me to catch up on lessons I had missed, so that when the first report came out, my form teacher simply said: 'Absence has hindered John's education'. You can say that again! During this time, some of the school facilities were still not up and running, in particular the gymnasia and playing fields. I'm not sure what happened to the girls, but in the case of us boys, we had to change for PE in the open cloakrooms in the Heavy Skills block and trudge snake-like to the Little Heath Football Club's playing field some half a mile away (it's still there unchanged). By the time we arrived, there was hardly time to play before we had to trudge back again. No showers, of course, so for the rest of the day the mud on knees and elbows would slowly solidify into cakes, to eventually fall off.

Reflecting on the school curriculum then, from the present standpoint and the development of education, leaves me with the conclusion that at that time it was a bit rudderless: trying to shake off the ethos of the 1942 Education Act by resisting the secondary modern 'failures' of the Eleven Plus, and trying to emulate the grammar and public schools (ironically, I ended up as a teacher in both education systems for a brief time years later) but without the teaching expertise to do so. 'Child-Centred Education' trumpeted by the advocates was difficult for some of the teachers.

As mentioned previously there was great play on practical subjects at the expense of core subjects. This squeezed academic subjects – geography and history for example - along with the three sciences, although oddly French took up a chunk of the precious timetable for some obscure reason. English and mathematics were strictly structured. Fair enough for maths but the English language and literature teaching I found both confusing and perplexing which put me off for years to come. Grammar was taught via 'clause analysis' which was baffling and as for the set texts, they were quite unsuitable. For most of us grounded in Enid Blyton and popular comics, for example, it was a big jump into 'Allan Quartermain and Shakespeare's 'Midsummer Night's Dream'! The former, written in

1887, was old fashioned, irrelevant and impossible to relate to and the latter impenetrable and silly with Pucks, Fairies, and Bottom. Who on earth decided on these tomes?

I can look back and reflect that I enjoyed my time in the main. After settling in I'm afraid I have to own up to being not an ideal pupil. I got into trouble, experienced the cane a few times and spent too much time in detention. But after a while I sorted myself out and the lyrics of The Beatles 'Getting Better' song sums it up:

I used to get mad at my school
The teachers who taught me weren't cool
You're holding me down (ah-ah)
Turning me 'round
Filling me up with your rules

I've got to admit it's getting better
A little better all the time (it can't get no worse)
I have to admit it's getting better
It's getting better
Since you've been mine....

saw the light and knuckled down even if the choice of subjects taken earlier was a mistake. At that time when pupils ended the third year (year 0) a decision had to be made on the avenue ahead known as bias. From memory, among the possible subjects were Science, Literature, Commerce, Technical and 'General Studies' along with compulsory English, Maths and French with the aim of taking external GCSEs after 2 years. You had to pass a 'mock' exam to enter. If not, it was simply hard luck and this applied to a predominant proportion of pupils - after all the examination system had to be paid for out of taxes! There was no grading, just Pass or Fail, which was a bit severe. Another set was for those who had no intention of carrying on full-time education after they had reached fifteen years of age. Unlike now there was no choice of subjects outside these parameters, which might have helped administration but certainly didn't help the pupils.

The facilities and extra-curricular activities such as sport and drama were excellent and widened the enjoyment and experience of many young people including me. But this couldn't disguise the fact that core background subjects towards full-time education were at the expense of being urged into a working environment at the age of fifteen and sixteen but very few into further education.

At that time 3.4% of young people went on to university, in the main from public and grammar schools. The number is now in the region of 50% from all secondary education establishments. I cannot see that there has been a sudden surge of intelligence between then and now. The thought of a whole load of my generation never having been given the opportunity is nothing less than a tragedy. In 1960 the number of universities more than doubled from 22 to 45. Now there are over 90; 18 in London alone.

Some years later and with the help of 'Friends Reunited' I ended up organising a reunion to celebrate the fiftieth anniversary of the official opening of the school (which was held at the Palace of Westminster no less). I was able to inspect the admission register of the 194 entry of my year and it came home to me the number of my fellow pupils who were at orphanages. There were two - Chequers Mead and Northaw (ironically in Hertfordshire rather than Middlesex). I would guess that more than 10% of pupils came from there. So why such a large number? This was undoubtedly a result of WW2. Childbearing women with their husbands away from home fell into extra-marital relations, some with the newly arrived American GIs. Perhaps before hubby came home, the babies were whisked off to an orphanage rather than the wives having to face the consequences. Alternatively, some husbands found that the new offspring was difficult to live with or they simply couldn't afford an extra mouth to feed. Data suggests that every 15th child was illegitimate during the height of the war along with every 7th conceived outside marriage, but surely must be guesswork. Perhaps some husbands accepted the situation and learnt to live with it. The rather cruel jibe was that they were 'grudge babies' - someone had it in for them!

Looking back, it was with sadness that I left. As it turned out, the connection to the school remained for the rest of my life. I was a founder member of the Old Scholars Football Club when it was formed in the year I left and from this humble beginning it has morphed into the very successful Potters Bar Town FC, playing at the time of writing in the Isthmian Premier League. Through that club I was swept off my feet by the school gym mistress who joined the staff just after I left.

Eventually moving to a house opposite the school and like poacher becoming a gamekeeper I ended up as a governor of the school many years later. This long connection couldn't have been imagined when I entered the portals as a scared and bamboozled eleven year old kid, that's for sure.

Some thirty years after I left the school, I found myself supply teaching for a year in a public school at Haberdashers Askes. Putting aside the time from when I was at school, the lasting impression I had was that the privileged pupils were geared to management whereas at Mount Grace the only aim was to work on the 'shop floor'. Ambition for higher things simply didn't exist, during my school days.

ABOVE AVERAGE AT SPORT

The title at the top of the page is taken from a book about PG Wodehouse - one of my favourite authors. I was a bit of a wimp until the hormones kicked in, but then from my early teens thoroughly enjoyed many aspects of sport although without qualified support from my family, it must be said.

One of the first stirrings of my interest in competitive sport came in watching TV in 1954 when the Englishman Chris Chataway just beat the Russian Kuts in the 5000 metres for a new world record at the White City. Later at a more modest level lying on the grass and witnessing the older boys on Sports Day, I was simply caught up in the romance and desire to emulate and take part.

There was, however, a slight drawback - I could hold my own with my kindred spirits of sporting mates but couldn't escape the fact that though keen, I was a player who was just above being average. It didn't matter: I drew the very best out of myself which made the often-modest achievements particularly rewarding. This recreation malarkey began to surpass me at the expense of schoolwork. Sport in its widest sense took over - from athletics in the summer to team games in the winter.

To quote from my leaving testimonial from my school PE master, Ken Barrett: *'In my position as senior sports master... I must emphasize his great value to me as a sportsman. He has represented the School in Soccer, Rugby, Cricket, Tennis, Athletics and Basketball. In Rugby and Athletics, he was awarded Senior School Colours and represented the District in both these events'.*

That's the good bit and then the codicil:

'John would be the first to agree that his strongest point in games is not skill of a natural calibre. He is not a natural ball player. This, however, is more than made good by an excellent attitude of maturity, reliability and, above all, enthusiasm. Such enthusiasm has often inspired his team-mates to better efforts ... He was a founder member of the boat club and has been on Sailing and Skiing journeys ...'. Damned with faint praise, no wonder my schoolwork suffered!

My enthusiasm for sport carried on after leaving school, playing for Mount Grace Old Scholars very first football team that has now morphed under the banner of a very successful Potters Bar Town FC, the town Athletic Club along with the Boxing Club, and later the Crusaders and Chipping Barnet Cricket Clubs. Then later still joining Barnet Rugby Club and in my middle-age Squash and Brookman's Park Golf Club. The lasting mantra that mostly arose when taking part was: lose, try again, lose better. Or better still, as the poem *Alumnus* by the sportswriter Grantland Rice puts it: 'For when the One Great Scorer comes to mark against your name - not that you won or lost - but how you played the Game'. Yes, that'll do.

Caught up in the euphoria of England winning the football World Cup in 1966 a handful of people, including most notably Cllr Don Gregory, suggested the idea of a Sports Council for the town. All the existing sports clubs were invited to a meeting to discuss the idea. At the time I was the honorary secretary and a participant of the Potters Bar Athletic Club and I was keen on the idea; before I knew it I found myself on the committee. For the first time I was made painfully aware of the petty politics and bureaucracy that at times manifested itself in this newly created forum . As it happens it turned out to be fairly well run and the affiliated sports clubs in the town, in the main, welcomed our involvement. From being an active participant, I found myself to be an administrator. The one subject that was often raised was the lack of a Sports Hall.

At about that time in the early seventies, Dame Allice Owen School had acquired the land at the end of Dugdale Hill Lane in order to move from Islington. At the planning stage, Don and I met up with the governors at the Worshipful Company of Brewers at Aldermanbury Square in the city to find out whether they would be prepared to allow a 'joint provision' sports hall. The idea was to allow the general public to use the facilities in the evenings and weekends in exchange for the local council paying half of the design and construction costs. This made sense for full use of the facility and the principle was adopted by many Councils throughout the land at that time of joint use with educational establishments. The reorganisation of local government was approaching and a lot of them didn't want to hand over their reserves to someone else even though they became part of it! As a Sports Development Council it wasn't too difficult to persuade the Potters Bar Councillors to do the same and we managed to secure a promise of funds for the much-needed sports hall. Unfortunately, the governors of the school rejected the idea, later admitting that they had sufficient funds anyway and didn't need financial help. The truth is they wanted to keep their sports hall for the benefit of the school only without interference. In any case there was a body of opinion that the location wasn't ideal, being on the outskirts of town.

Undeterred we looked at an alternative location. Parkfield School (see page 50) or Mount Grace Lower School as it was known at that time was to be vacated and I put together a report to use this site as a sports hall along with ancillary facilities. It had a lot going for it. Surrounded by the existing cricket, football, tennis and bowls clubs nearby, it was slap bang in the middle of town. A submission was made to Potters Bar Council in March 1972, just before the above reorganisation of local authorities, urging consideration of this idea. Indeed, the London School of Architecture agreed to sponsor a competition between the students to design such a facility and the designs were displayed in Oakmere library. The organisers even asked me to judge the entries! I cannot recall what the prize was, though.

It made sense to centralise all these existing sports clubs along with their facilities in one principal place and there was a much better location than Furzefield towards the edge of town. After some debate the Council rejected this proposal and a unique opportunity was lost. The argument was the expense of staffing two separate recreational facilities - the existing swimming pool on one hand and a sports hall on the other.

As an aside and on the subject of the Parkfield area, it has always been a regret to my mind that the old Ladbroke School in the High Street (now a listed building) was not converted and used as a civic building by the public of Potters Bar. It would have made an excellent meeting place with the interior converted into a public library and perhaps a museum too. Extending the idea with an avenue leading to the recreational facilities of the bowls, tennis, cricket and football clubs and exposing St Mary's Church along with the church hall rather than them being hidden away would have created a splendid and agreeable sort of town square. I approached the Council with this very suggestion after receiving encouraging responses to my letter published in the local paper. Sadly, it withered on the vine - the

65

Council and Planners wouldn't even discuss it. I talk about a 'Town Centre' (or lack of it) in another chapter.

As it happens, I was engaged by the PBUDC anyway to design a sports hall next to the swimming pool. The design was approved and the budget accepted. The problem was that the newly formed Hertsmere Borough Council wanted to take over and conduct the project 'in house' since the officers wanted to create an architects' department. The net result was that I was kicked into touch, the scheme grew like topsy and was delayed for a considerable time. Still, it now exists having been upgraded and I like to think I helped to be the vanguard of creating it. By the way, the said architects' department along with a selfish, scheming head of this department bent on empire building didn't last long and soon disappeared along with the brief.

Still, after all these battles and shenanigans and many delays, eventually a sports hall was built at Furzefield and has become a facility used by many some from out of town - of which the town can be justly proud. As the battle-weary trailblazer, I can sit back truly satisfied for a job well done.

HOME-GROWN RECREATION

Being a member of the 'war baby' generation, most of the time we made our own entertainment whilst growing up. There were none of the myriad forms of amusements now available for youngsters to keep them occupied. The fifties were grey and austere. Unlike these days there weren't many sports clubs that catered for youngsters. Sport and recreation outside school was organised or more accurately thrown together amongst ourselves. A lot of the time in my misspent youth - like most kids I imagine - was spent outdoors in all weathers.

Chaotic football games took place without a referee - some of which went on for hours or until it got dark. Jumpers were set down as goalposts and sides selected by self-appointed captains (one of whom was usually the boy who owned the ball). Naturally the numbers on each side were determined by those who had turned up – anything between six and twenty aside. As mentioned earlier unless boys (girls didn't play footy then) were taken to watch professional football there was no way of knowing the finer points of play. Other, that is, than once a year when the Cup Final was shown on black and white TV. The Football Association and League refused to show games including internationals live, afraid that crowds would stay away. Complete nonsense as we now know given the big crowds that attend top league matches despite the TV coverage. There weren't even TV highlights such as 'Match of the Day'.

It didn't stop us playing or collecting pictures of famous footballers, however, and I recall sticking my collection on the bedroom wall without a clue who they were. It didn't stay there for long as my father instructed me to take them down and thus avoid pinholes in the plaster! In the summer it was cricket which we had a better idea how to play since 5-day tests were on television. The coverage was restricted to a static camera at one end, so for half the overs all you saw was the wicket keeper's backside! I somehow won a Len Hutton-autographed Gradidge 'Harrow' bat in a competition which was freely used by everyone. My younger brother used to bowl to me down the narrow driveway in front of the garage at home. He started his run up the other side of the road.

Those of us who had a bike would peddle furiously off road, around Oakmere Park. Setting up the cycle with 'cow horn' handlebars and turning round the back wheel so that it was fixed rather than being on a ratchet, we would set out on a determined route through the undergrowth and round the trees whilst keeping a look-out for the park keeper. Without knowing it, we had given birth to cross country as well as BMX racing which has featured in the Olympics ever since the 2008 games in Beijing.

Anyone who was able to get hold of old pram wheels would make a trolley. With a short scaffold plank one pair was fixed to the back and the other pair to a separate piece of wood at the front attached with a bolt for steering. This was achieved by string either side as well as resting the feet on the axle. The only way of stopping was to wear out the heels on your shoes by using them to brake, before crashing into a convenient wall or hedge. Cuts and bruises were the norm and we proudly held them up like medieval battle scars.

Roads were almost deserted when compared with the grown-up Scalextric rat-runs we seem to accept now. Dad owned a modest car at various times, otherwise he used to cycle to and from work, but we were no different to similar families of my generation. We didn't go on a summer holiday to the seaside so spent the vacation just being with mates up the park (see above). Other than, that is, when he acquired a second-hand Morris Standard 8 and we set off to stay with his uncle and aunt who ran a dairy farm in Masham - a village in the west riding of Yorkshire – James Herriot's country and famous for 'Old Peculiar' and the Black Sheep Beer. I loved being there..

Parents were notable by their absence when we played team games Today, of course, the opposite is mostly true. As an example, my old rugby club runs well organised mini and junior rugby on Sunday mornings for a huge number of boys (and some girls) from the age of five upwards. Dads stand on the touchline – if they're not coaching – to encourage the youngsters. In my day it didn't happen. I would hope that parents were just as devoted at that time but in the 1950s it was simply a different culture Fathers generally were very different, more detached than the present generation and saw themselves in general as upright, dutiful and sensible doubtless ingrained from a legacy from the Victorian times and th discipline of military service. The reticence of that generation of men, their stiff upper lip and stoicism were hard for us as small boys to break through. They talked about the war a bit but not about themselves and certainly wasn't a boy's best friend or his fun buddy.

In the case of my own father, I would guess on reflection it may have been the fact that his own father had died when he was about seven years of age because of the Spanish Flu pandemic in 1919; ironic, as it turned out, as he had survived the horrors of the Great War that had recently finished. The pandemic was caused by the H1N1 virus with genes of avian origin and spread to almost every corner of the world. Thus, my father didn't have a 'father figure' of his own. This must have been a devastating time: young adults between 20 and 30 years old were particularly affected and the disease struck and progressed quickly. The onset was incredibly fast - those who had been fine and healthy at breakfast could be dead by tea-time. Within hours of feeling the first symptoms of fatigue, fever and headache, some victims would rapidly develop pneumonia and start turning blue, signalling a shortage of oxygen. They would then struggle for air until they suffocated to death. During the pandemic of 1918/19, a quarter of the British population was affected. The death toll was 228,000 in Britain alone. More people died of influenza in that single year than in the four years of the Black Death Bubonic Plague from 1347 to 1351. It puts into perspective the advances in medical science in treating Covid19. We should give thanks for the vast number who survived and count ourselves fortunate that the scientists and research chemists came up trumps.

My father's reserve must have been a consequence of having no experience of having a father figure of his own during his formative years. It must have been equally devastating for his mother to lose a 30 year old husband and look after not only a young boy but also a six month old baby without the help of any sort of benefit system. Hard times indeed.

ORGANISED RECREATION

The title 'Teenager' didn't exist until the 1950s. From the end of the War young people dressed just like their parents due in the main, I suppose, to the austerity at that time. But then things slowly changed in the middle of the decade. Doubtless influenced by America in both popular music and films, there was an upsurge of a benign, in the main, rebellion of the generation.

Jeans made an appearance and have been with us ever since. Teddy Boys were created in city conurbations, wearing their Edwardian jackets and drainpipe trousers. Girls dressed in sleeveless blouses and flared skirts with layers of petticoats underneath. In Potters Bar the fashions were a little watered down. At school luminous socks to go with the narrow drainpipe trousers for boys were banned and if the hem of the skirt didn't touch the ground when the girls kneeled, they were told in no uncertain terms to make the necessary adjustments. I'm not sure how this was achieved.

Out of school there were all sorts of clubs in the town. In my case, I was involved with the Scouting movement and in particular 'First Little Heath & Potters Bar Sea Scouts', which sadly no longer exists. It was great fun. There was a sort of discipline, and it was run on military lines. We wore sailors' jumpers and hats although never went near the sea and sea shanty never passed our lips.

Sports-wise, it was The Crusaders and Little Heath football clubs along with the cricket club and two tennis clubs, but these only catered for adults there was no room for youngsters. If they were short of players and you were persistent and keen enough, you were thrown in at the deep end. Potters Bar Boxing Club and the Athletic Club in the summer were exceptions and I believe the table tennis club was similar. As for swimming, the nearest pool was the Finchley Lido - two bus rides involving a journey of over an hour each way - which was unheated and outdoors. A smaller outdoor pool was at San Marina (which doubled up as a restaurant) in South Mimms which shut up in the mid-fifties.

Other than sport, it was pretty dire seeking out recreation and meeting up with your mates and of course, hopefully, with tag-along gals. The Council ran a youth club at Elm Court which mainly consisted of playing table tennis. There was a record player to listen to but not to dance to; the best you could hope for was a drink of orange and awaiting your turn to play table tennis. There was another youth club at King Charles the Martyr opposite and the general opinion was that if it was run by the church it wasn't going to be a great deal of fun.

But oh dear, it didn't suit those of us who saw ourselves as the Beat Generation and what we were witnessing wasn't like what was coming out of the US and being featured in the glossy magazines and films. We had to go out of the town to dances in Southgate and Tottenham - but this was expensive and it took a long time travelling by bus. Nearer home was the North Twenty dance studios above Burton Taylors in the High Street Barnet. There was a disco, a bit of ballroom dancing (the owners would show off swirling round the dance floor for a 'spot' much to our amusement) but in the main good old pop records of the day. No bar only soft drinks of course, but it was an opportunity to cut a rug with partner you fancied from a distance. You tried, if possible, to set yourself up with that special one you had your eye on for the 'Last Waltz'.

Once a year the 'Youth Fete' took place at the ground, where Potters Bar Town Football Club now plays in the summer. By definition it involved lots of teenagers - it was great fun, but this was just one day of the year. Also, twice a year there was a visit of the funfair which was erected in front of Parkfield Park. The latest pop records blared over the dodgems and with your mates one just used to hang around eyeing up that which took your fancy in the hope of a response. There were pubs of course but youngsters were forbidden to enter until they were 'adults' and I don't think anybody had any desire to do so anyway. The only real entertainment was the Ritz cinema but more of that later.

THE DARK SIDE

It is understandable, I suppose, that we tend to look back at our childhood and youth through rose-coloured glasses, but there was a sinister side. Never talked about or shared with parents, other people in authority or highlighted in the media as it is now. One of the most refreshing elements of the present day is that it is recognised and help is available. The fact that it exists at all is now well-known and is mostly addressed.

This is hard to admit, but I was abused as a young child by a male relative. I couldn't understand his encouragement to join him in bed when he took his afternoon 'nap' so that he could relate his time during the war. I was scared and confused and didn't have the courage to relate these horrible experiences to anyone. I have kept them to myself until now.

Corporal punishment in school by bullying teachers was a common occurrence. Some seemed to enjoy it. Worse though was my experience of a female English teacher when I was about fourteen. I was often chastised by her for, justifiable misdemeanours but instead of being put in detention I would be instructed to see her after school. These experiences were most confusing for a boy who was slowly discovering the usual hormones manifesting themselves at that time. She would cross-examine my feelings of the opposite sex which I simply didn't understand until eventually she made a pass. I pushed her away and simply ran off. After that she made my life a misery to such an extent that the following term, I was pushed down two classes and since it was the beginning of the GCE curriculum the following autumn term, it took me the two following terms to get back to where I started and should have been all along. A consequence was that I wasn't entered for the exam at the end of the fifth form which had a detrimental effect on later studies in the sixth form. She left before this happened and to this day I curse that I had the misfortune of being taught (in more ways than one) by this awful predatory female.

There were certainly boys I knew at school who were somewhat effeminate or at least didn't join in the games the rest of us played. They were bullied a bit but in the main left alone. The handle 'gay' meant something quite different in those days! When I was about ten years old we would spend most of our free time in Oakmere Park, a rumour once went around that there was this bloke who would pay half a crown (12¹/₂ p) for any of us boys to spend 'time' with him. We were told he was a 'homo' which I didn't understand. The only word I knew was 'Omo' which was a washing powder. How naive we were!

Worst of all was the leader of the First Little Heath and Potters Bar Sea Scout Troop. He was a sinister odd man made worse by the fact that his son was also a member and seemed to follow in his father's creepy footsteps. It came to a head at a camp when this very son acted in a strange and abrasive manner seemingly with the encouragement of our revered leader. As a group we didn't know how to handle this, for no other reason than that there was no-one to go to. Suddenly, they both resigned: none of us knew how or why but we all were relieved to see the back of them both.

JUST SUPPOSING

Supposing that Potters Bar Town Football Club had just won the FA Cup - better still the European Cup - or a resident had just won gold at the Olympic Games. Naturally there would have to be a procession through the town on an open-topped bus in order to acknowledge the cheering crowds, but which route to take and more importantly where would it end?

On the balcony of the Town Hall in the centre of town? Er no, there is no balcony, not even steps, or come to that a Town Hall or even a Civic Centre. The centre of the town is also a problem. The car park in front of Sainsbury's, perhaps, or maybe the carved tree in the middle of Parkfield Park?

Actually, there was a procession through the town of an Olympic hero. His name was Johnny Wright. He was a nineteen year old middleweight boxer who won the silver medal in the 1948 Olympic Games in London, defeated by Laszlo Papp of Hungary, he was in effect a professional fighter, over Johnny's amateur status and went on to win the following two Olympic golds at Helsinki and Melbourne. Johnnie paraded through his hometown in an open car and was presented with a Carriage Clock by the town council on the stage of the Ritz Cinema. He retired from boxing some ve years later and ended up as landlord of The Fallow Buck Inn (sadly no nger a pub) close to Whitewebbs House near Enfield where the said ock was proudly displayed above the bar. I remember Johnnie Wright ing a jolly 'mine host' with a battered nose who was no longer a iddleweight, more a sumo wrestler. He had a Great Dane dog who was big he could put its head over the bar without having to jump up.

d there is the rub. There is no centre of the town and the Civic Offices e located miles away in Borehamwood. The reason there is no centre is at there are two 'High Streets' with houses in between. The original one the east was an ancient road -The Great North Road no less. The word

'High' is a good description for the land either side falls away leaving a sort of ridge. Darkes Lane exists in main because of the railway station. The train route to and from Kings Cross had to go via a tunnel at the top end as the adjacent ground was too high and a cutting was too expensive and impractical for a station.

So where is the hub of the town then? It could be the four-way junction of the High Street, The Causeway, Cotton Road and Hatfield Road. Historically it has legs. Within a stone's throw of each other used to be the hospital in Richmond Road, the police station, the village hall and the telephone exchange, not forgetting the Green Man pub now all gone. A bit chaotic now with a maelstrom of traffic though to attract a congregation unless we climbed over the fence onto Morven open space and joined the cows!

As a postscript about what might have been, apparently there was a proposal for a tube line to be constructed in the early thirties which would have joined the end of the Northern Line at High Barnet to the end of the Piccadilly Line at Cockfosters via Potters Bar. The station would have been located next to the bus garage in front of Parkfield Park. Was the town's population too small to justify it? Not really. The underground stations at Amersham (pop 17,700) and Croxley (pop 12,000) are below Potters Bar (currently at 22,000). The distance and sheer logistics along with the expense would have been too big a challenge of course. The line would have had to be via tunnels presumably through the town and a viaduct over Stag Hill. Still, it would have made a huge change to the town, of that there is no doubt.

READING

Education has produced a vast population able to read but unable to distinguish what is worth reading, said G M Trevelyan, so with that in mind it has to be admitted that literature for youngsters was pretty limited at home and the main sources of reading material were comics. There was a small satellite two-roomed library near where I lived (now demolished) next to Oakmere House with a small children's section. Most of the books were fairly dog-eared with mainly Enid Blyton editions – 'The Famous Five' and 'Secret Seven' – all very middle class. These adventures reflected a world that didn't align with our more modest existence, not helped by 'Just William' books - the hero lived in a large detached house with a 'maid of all things'. Worse still was 'Billy Bunter,' set in a public school, in which the fat owl of the fourth remove was quite an alien world. The 'Bash Street Kids' in 'The Beano' comic were easier to identify with, even though the teacher swanned around in a gown and mortar board! The librarians didn't have much of a clue - I recall asking whether they had 'Twenty Thousand Leagues under the Sea' and was told to go away and find out the name of the author!

Thus, we looked forward to and avidly consumed 'The Beano' and 'Dandy', 'Film Fun' and 'Radio Fun'. There are not so many comics nowadays unless you include modern national newspapers such as 'The Star', 'The Sun' and 'Daily Mirror'! Children's comics such as 'The Rover', 'The Hotspur', and 'The Magnet' usually contained a mixture of adventure stories presented as text rather than strip cartoons. Later the 'Tiger' comic featuring 'Roy of the Rovers' who played for Melchester Rovers football team appeared. His name is legion for no other reason than he is sometimes mentioned even to this day. Another strip cartoon worth mentioning was 'The Broons' and 'Our Wullie' annuals sent to me from relatives in Scotland which took a while to understand, with their phonetic texts.

Then on 14 April 1950 the first issue of 'Eagle' hit the stands. Twice the size of other comics, printed on glossy paper rather than newsprint, it was a seminal periodical for boys (a sister comic followed later for girls based on a similar

EAGLE ANNUAL
1951-1959

principle entitled without much inspiration 'Girl'). The cartoonist for 'Dan Dare – Pilot of the Future' on the front cover was Frank Hampson (followed later by Martin Aitchison), beautifully drawn with meticulous attention to detail, all in vivid colours. We kids were thrilled by the square-jawed Dan Dare (Pilot of the Future) British spaceman's weekly exploits, and his struggles with The Mekon.

Despite its relatively high price compared to other comics, it was an immediate success; eight of the twenty pages were presented in vivid colour and it was designed to entertain as well as educate with such characters as Cavendish Brown, Harris Tweed (geddit?), Jack O'Lantern, Riders of the Range, PC 49 and Luck of the Legion. Each issue also featured a centre spread full-colour cutaway mechanical illustration of, for example, the inner workings of a railway locomotive or a battleship.

We are now blessed with a fine library near to the original behind the medical centre, totally unrecognisable from the old one. It was built on the spot where a fighter plane was shot down, the wreckage of which we kids used to clamber over playing at being pilots before it was taken away. Having said that, I always thought that the best place for a library would be the old Ladbrook School fronting the High Street (mentioned earlier). Along with the library the rear part of the buildings could have accommodated the Potters Bar Museum rather than it being squeezed into its present situation in Wyllyotts Manor.

THE MUSIC REVOLUTION

A treasured signed copy of the programme. I mentioned to one of the artistes that as a kid I had sent off a postal order to see them perform and filled it in by mistake which led to it being returned. Hence the message.

On the evening of Monday 29 October 2001, 'The Comets' performed their last show in the UK at Wyllyotts Centre, Potters Bar. Never in my wildest dreams did I think that I would ever witness live one of the legends of rock and roll. There they were, the very band - or at least those who were left - who backed Bill Haley, the Godfather who arguably started the pop revolution in the mid fifties. Little did I imagine then that many years later that Bill Haley's 'Comets' would perform in Potters Bar! Memories came flooding back; it was simply the best musical happening that an old rocker had ever experienced. I still can't believe that a band that rocked the world would find their way to our modest little town.

There are moments, by sheer chance, that peoples' lives happen to coincide with seismic cultural moments. War, pestilence, revolutions, moments when the world suddenly changes. A new generation of young people from this country slowly emerged from the dreary cash-strapped fifties who had some money to spend for the first time and the media soon found a new name for them. Simply put they were called teenagers and I was one of them – it was an extraordinary coincidence that I became a teenager at the age of thirteen in 1955, the year which really saw the birth of rock and roll.

By chance at about that time, I was chosen to join other English Scouts in an exchange arrangement with Boy Scouts of America who were the sons of military personnel billeted in occupied Southern Germany. Not quite America per se but near enough. It didn't quite work out as I hoped as the boy I was allocated turned out to be an absolute spoiled brat. But staying for two weeks in an army camp complex in Wiesbaden and experiencing how the other half lived lifted the scales from my eyes. The environment was so different from the drab, closeted, cash-strapped existence at home. There were supermarkets, bowling alleys, hamburger joints and coffee bars along with the freedom to do what we wanted. It was so very different from the sombre UK. Most exciting of all was the music played on AFN Radio along with jukeboxes in coffee bars. I was sold on rock and roll.

The man who started it all was Bill Haley (see previous page) closely followed by Elvis, Little Richard, Jerry Lee Lewis, Fats Domino, Buddy Holly, et al. With backbeat percussion, it was music which was loud, lively and so different from popular music at that time, geared to the younger generation who cried out for something different.

This was all happening mainly in the USA of course but by golly, it was damned difficult to listen to this new form of music via the radio. Staid BBC wasn't interested in playing pop music and the only way you could listen to it was by tuning into Radio Luxembourg, a crackly programme from the

Grand Duchy. The BBC just didn't want to know. From what I understand there was a dispute between America and the UK on music rights so the only music you could hear on the BBC was live band and orchestral music. The pop records we were listening to on Radio Luxembourg were in the main from America, although Tommy Steele tried hard. There was a programme on this station between 11 o'clock and midnight on a Sunday evening when they played the 'Top 20' which I used to listen to avidly in bed, keeping the sound down as much as possible so as not to awaken my younger brother who shared the bedroom with me. At first, the list was based on the sale of sheet music rather than record sales which skewed the pop scene somewhat. For weeks on end, I seem to remember 'The Dam Busters March' being at number 18! It eventually changed to disc sales although it is rumoured that record producers would find out which of the record stores were used to collect data and skewed the market to buying their own discs.

Sometimes there were British bands and singers that imitated these records, but they were pretty naff. **It got better as time went on eventually leading** to The Beatles, The Kinks and The Rolling Stones (but not, repeat not, Cliff Richard) although this was some time later. Even so, rock was accessible - something that could be played and enjoyed without education or training and it was something the coming generation would understand although their parents found it bewildering. It was potent and different.

An example is the classic 1956 rock and roll film 'The Girl Can't Help It' which begins with the main character flicking the screen and the narrow frame becoming much wider; then the black and white images turn to colour followed by the sound of Little Richard singing 'Tutti Frutti', the intro being **A WOP BOP A LOO BOP A LOP BAM BOOM** This outrageous disc hit the turntables at the start of R & R and changed the world. The reaction of teenagers such as me at that time was, I imagine, just like that of Paul McCartney and John Lennon. They knew they had heard something that was true and that there was no going back. To the latter in particular it seemed that everything in his life to that point had been a set up for a ride on this magic carpet. Boy, I was lucky to join at just the right age and time of this vanguard of something special.

Mind you, a mention should be made of a genre that ran parallel for a brief time in the late fifties battling with rock music in the UK. That was traditional (trad) jazz and skiffle. The former was too hard to play and appeared to attract a following that seemed to be keen to keep it to themselves; in any case the tunes were a bit 'samey'. Skiffle was simpler since acoustic guitars were cheaper than electric ones which needed an amplifier and had a tea chest 'base' and a washboard rhythm, it was cheap and anyone could play. I even had a go myself although unable to read music or play a note - the only instrument I was trusted with was the tea chest although if there was a piano handy, I could vamp from watching my father play. We even went in for a talent show at the Ritz cinema but didn't feature in the winner's enclosure sadly. Skiffle didn't last long not surprisingly, and the pioneer Lonnie Donegan sold his soul to silly songs like 'My Old Man's a Dustman'. Some made it of course - don't forget John Lennon's and Paul McCartney's first band was a skiffle group.

Records of pop music could be bought at Delmar's music shop in Darkes Lane. The old fragile shellac 10 inch at 78 rpm were slowly replaced by 7 inch at 45 rpm vinyl along with 12 inch LPs at 33.3 rpm. (the record player used to cater for all three). Newspapers would publish weekly Top Twenty Hits which we avidly followed. If one of the records got into the top twenty, then we saved up to buy it. The records were expensive, though A 7" record was 6 shillings and 4 pence (32p) and an LP was over £2.00 A disc equated to about the amount of money you could earn carrying heavy bag by caddying at Potters Bar Golf Club! Conveniently the record shop was opposite the entrance. Thus, struggling round the golf course for four hours as a caddy with a heavy bag equated to 3 minutes of pop music!

My mate and I came up with a wheeze to use the redundant old british shellac records and earn a few bob by putting these records over an upturned bowl in an oven, the heat of which would melt them into as trays. There was a design fault, however, that we had forgotten about. the hole in the middle where the fag ash fell through.

The discs wore out with continual playing on the Dancette record player and to avoid the needle jumping we would delicately balance coins over the stylus causing the grooves to become deeper and the music slowly distorted. But hey, so what, it was groovy (in more ways than one) man!

It is interesting that L.P. vinyl records have become increasingly popular and in consequence a valuable opportunity lost! Although I still have a few somewhere, I think.

We've gone from storing our music on Bakelite brittle records to vinyl to tape cassettes and on to CDs, MP3 files and finally to streaming music from the cloud. Before all these innovations, shelves were stacked with heavy records. Fast forward to the present and your average teenager has, in their hand, the ability to stream practically any song that has ever been recorded. Thousands of such songs blobbed on something the size of a fingernail or stored somewhere up in the clouds!

Rock pervaded both an age revolution and classroom revolution. It didn't act on its own of course for without post-war prosperity and demographic change there would have been none of the teen culture which I experienced. The 1957 decision to abolish National Service was important in leading to a feeling of freedom and power among young people in Britain.

There was a little bit of regret in my case as I just missed National Service and I think I probably would have enjoyed being part of it (after all I had to listen to my father regaling his experiences in the Second World War so I might have been able to respond and identify a little). Also I would have been able to shake off the shackles of being imprisoned at home: leaving as a boy, coming home a man, and so on. The present generation is able to do the same as it has the opportunity of university life away from home. My generation missed out really. But then, without this revolution during the sixties, some of the vanguard groups such as the Beatles would have been doing National Service!

PUTTING ON THE RITZ

When I was a youngster, along with most of my contemporaries, it was almost compulsory to go to the Saturday morning pictures at the town cinema. It was known as Ritz KKK which meant the Kiddies Kine Klub - so they obviously couldn't spell. Two queues were formed outside beforehand with the few girls on one side and the boys on the other. The girls were let in first followed by the boys and were kept strictly separated by the manager Frank Seymour.

Frank Seymour used to run the cinema on strict military lines when it came to kids. He was always impeccably dressed in a dinner jacket complete with bow tie with his wife squashed into a kiosk to the left as you entered the foyer to dish out the entrance tickets. She was exquisitely dressed to go along with the manager's image and looked a little like the incarnation of Barbara Cartland, made up to the nines with permed blue rinsed hair whatever time of day it was and dressed in what seemed to be a ball gown.

The entrance charge was the princely sum of sixpence (2.5p). The manager obviously saw himself as a sort of sentinel and if he suspected any of the young boys entering had any form of armoury about their person they were fleeced and the weapons (such as catapults, peashooters and elastic band 'guns') thrown into a large tea chest. These weapons could be claimed after the show was over but it didn't take long for the more astute of us to leave a little bit early so we could snaffle the better missile launchers.

The programme was much the same each week: there was a short cowboy film or Laurel and Hardy followed by a limited library of cartoons. There was community singing when the words would come up on the screen with a bouncing ball over each word and everybody who could read joined in with gusto and a cacophony of out-of-tune noise. There was an organ, but I don't remember it being played. The finale was seemingly a never-ending serial where the rather overweight hero in grainy black and white would get into all sorts of scrapes at the end of each episode but always managed to get out of them the following week. As an example, I recall one occasion when he was firmly bound and trapped in a locked car that was heading at breakneck speed towards the edge of a high cliff, flew over the top and crashed on to the shore below. How on earth could he get out of it? You simply had to come back the following week to find out how he could possibly escape certain death. We watched anxiously the following Saturday when to everyone's amazement we discovered that he had just managed to break free of his bonds and jump out of the car door at the last second before it descended on its journey to oblivion below. We looked at each other in amazement since we must have forgotten that part of the film the previous week. I don't remember it ever ending - perhaps it was on a loop.

There was an interval when you could purchase ice cream if you had the money. The manager, if he was in a good mood, used to climb up on to the stage and organise a sort of talent show for anybody who wanted to perform. There were not many takers and generally it was the same precocious kids who had appeared previously. Sometimes young girls would get up wearing tap shoes and clack away with their well-rehearsed routine. There was, I recall, a yo-yo competition when it became all the rage to play with them. Then there was an occasion when the manager announced that if it was anybody's birthday they could come up on the stage and receive a little present, usually very small sweets (still on ration). The following week there were more kids whose birthday it was and the week after that almost the entire audience lined up for their gift. The organiser therefore decided to bring this wheeze to an end by replacing it with a lucky number on the entrance ticket which nobody seemed to win since they were usually chucked away.

The Ritz Cinema was one of several 'Ritz' cinemas built and designed by Major W J King. It was opened on 8 October 1934 with Eddie Cantor in 'Roman Scandals' and Ralph Bellamy in 'One is Guilty'. It was leased to Associated British Cinemas but became independent not long after.

As you can see it had a fortress-style exterior described as 'American Jazz'. Seating in the auditorium was in ground floor stalls and a mezzanine upper level. There was a central dome in the ceiling, which was illuminated around its inner rim. The Ritz Cinema was equipped originally with a Compton manual organ which ascended when required (mainly to sell ice creams I suspect) from the orchestra pit. There was also a fully equipped stage, which was used on rare occasions. The cinema had on the first floor at the front what was described as a ballroom and a tea lounge although I never saw either of these functions being used.

The Ritz Cinema Potters Bar.

or the adult audience weekdays comprised two programmes - Monday o Wednesday and then Thursday to Saturday. These films had been shown reviously by the main distributors such as the Odeon or Gaumont. The ackage was a continuous programme so you could go in at any time and ry to catch up when the films came round again. If you were in the mood r didn't have anything else to do you could watch them all over again. On undays a tame old film was shown in the late afternoon presumably to eflect the Sabbath.

ompared with today there wasn't much easily accessible entertainment r young people to go to locally other than the flea pit. I for one will ways look back with fond recollections indelibly sealed into my memory.

was impossible to go into a local pub under the age of eighteen even if ou only drank a cordial or Coca Cola. As mentioned previously youth ubs weren't much cop. These were usually run by the local church in eary places such as a scout hut. I do recall going to a youth club run by ng Charles the Martyr located in Mutton Lane. The entertainment ovided consisted of sipping orange juice whilst waiting to take turns to y table tennis.

The vicar and his obsequious assistants would mosey around with small talk suggesting visiting the church the following Sunday and making sure that the sexes were kept firmly apart. There was music admittedly but never a record in the top twenty and certainly not rock 'n roll which might lead to, God forbid, dancing! It was not for cool dudes like me and my mates. Accordingly, there was no alternative than to go to the Ritz cinema. If you had enough money you would go up into the balcony and hopefully smooch in the back row with your latest squeeze.

It was a rolling programme of two films. Going in at say 6.30pm on a Saturday night, the main feature was seen before the second feature film, usually a cowboy film with Randolph Scott. In this way you could avoid the crowds and nab a back seat upstairs taking care to avoid the doleful gaze of Frank in his dicky tie. On the back of the seats in the front there were ashtrays which allowed smoking to take place and if there was a sufficient audience puffing away it used to affect whether you could see the screen clearly or not. Worse than that, however, was if it had been raining outside when the steam would come off creating a haze. In any event, there was no air conditioning! As time went on the cinema did begin to become a bit sophisticated by bringing in Cinemascope widescreen. I recall the first film to be shown in this format was 'The Robe' starring Richard Burton and Jean Simmons.

Rumour has it that on the last occasion a film was shown, a man was discovered lying across three seats in the stalls and despite pleas from the usherette not to do so, he didn't move. The manager was called and faced with the same dilemma, asked where he was from. His muffled reply was 'From the gallery'.

As competition from TV increased it meant that the cinema struggled and in consequence had to diversify occasionally. Thus, it bought in 'All-Professional Wrestling'. A ring was set up on the stage and the snorting performers used to put together a show. So that the audience could view the action, the ring itself was set on the stage at a slight slope to face the audience so that the warriors used to spend most of their time trying not to slither down into the pit below. A poignant occasion was when the former middleweight boxing champion of the world Randolph Turpin performed to earn a crust and fight illness which took him at an early age. Finally, 'rock and roll' arrived in the form of the newly formed band 'T

Who' whose piece de resistance was demolishing their instruments at the end of their performance. Not long after this, the cinema experienced the same fate.

It was closed on 1 July 1967 after 33 years of a rocky commercial existence with a film of Morecambe & Wise in 'That Riviera Touch' and James Stewart in 'Shenandoah'. It had been sold to Tesco Supermarkets the previous April and was subsequently demolished (fortunately the Compton organ was rescued). Such a shame.

SECRET AND HIDDEN

It is remarkable that a town which hasn't any notable places to see or experience for that matter, along with not much of a history, it does however, have a chunk of land which is quite astonishing and of which most of the local population have never heard or even know exists. It is a cave and not a modest one either. Near and beneath a very ordinary farm between Potters Bar and South Mimms there is a series of gigantic caverns which until recently had lain hidden since the First World War. From the surface you would never guess what lies below: only three narrow vertical shafts provide access to the vast underground chambers which were discovered almost by accident. These include a collapsed shaft large enough to accommodate horses and carts.

The caverns make up what is a huge chalk mine. A breath-taking testament to labourers who spent their entire lives wielding pickaxes by candlelight during the 19th century to supply raw materials of calcium carbonate and flint to the building trade. The mine consists of more than 1,132 feet (345 metres) of known tunnels up to 40 feet high and 32 feet wide (12.2 x 9.7 metres) and is one of the largest unsupported short mines anywhere in the world - just reflect on that - representing a volume of chalk exceeding 7,700 cubic metres. And yet there are few records of this. The reason? Simply good old-fashioned profit and tax evasion - a mine was a very taxable asset many years ago but a 'well' wasn't. A search through the records of nearby County Hall will reveal that only a 'well' is listed for the area, which was free of tax.

Among those who do know of the mine's precise location, there are rumours that the excavations are much larger. A surface pond indicates subsidence over a second mine and the entire field behind the farm is pitted with hollows suggesting a gigantic system of tunnels below. Now, geologists may argue otherwise, claiming that chalk is too soft and unstable to support such excavations, but the miners were jolly cunning. How? Well, the tunnels were started close to the surface and then the labourers would work their way down into the floor deeper and deeper to create the shape of a huge church vault or catacomb to give structural stability. This can be seen in large old buildings of the Middle Ages - the roofs and wall openings are curved at the top. The curves of the roofs mirrored the ecclesiastical buildings by trial and error, but they worked. The bending moments and stress diagrams used by post-industrial structural engineers and later backed up by computer programmes to mirror the shape prove its undeniable strength. These vaults were emptied of some 23,000 tonnes of chalk but stand firm as they did in the 1800s.

By all accounts, there is graffiti on the roof of the youngest tunnel recording the assumed last day of mining on 17 April 1912. There are other carvings apparently, some of which show the mining agent who wasn't particularly popular. This wasn't unusual in those times of non-union labour. The miners hated their agents who paid as little as they could get away with. Legend has it that one of the last miners - a William Rowson - had set light to the agent's house killing him, his wife and children along with destroying the records relating to the mine. There is no record of him being charged though. Scratched into a wall is an illustration of a burning house with a stick cartoon mining agent grimly waving his twiggy arms in the flames alongside the initials W R.

But that was in the past, so why is it not possible for the great unwashed to visit this extraordinary edifice?

It's bats. By this I mean real bats. As is well known, bats are a protected species - particularly Natterer's and Daubenton's bats - who use the tunnel system as winter quarters. The 'Herts of Middlesex Bat Group' spent over £6,000 some time ago on the mine's entrances along with clearing shafts to improve air circulation to the tunnels. It seems a shame that because of these little creatures we, the public, are denied access to the tunnels and caves to wonder at their morbid and mysterious history unless we join the bat group. Still, while development and intensive agriculture increase the threats to the bats' long term survival above ground, they at least have a secure retreat in the bowels of man's bygone excavation even if we can't join them. Mind you, I suppose health and safety would probably rear its head to protect the bats and prevent the public visiting a potentially dangerous environment. On the other hand, it would work quite well as a nuclear fallout shelter as long as room was available for the Batmobile...

On the matter of nuclear fallout, the other mysterious building isn't in Potters Bar exactly but along the A1000 near Brookmans Park - you can't miss it, being two storeys high and surrounded by tall aerials and huge communication dishes. It is rumoured that it goes down four floors into a 'fallout' bunker, the reason being that if a nuclear attack occurred the first targets would be transmitting stations such as this, so in the event of the big bang - pop goes dear old Potters Bar along with Brookmans Park on day one. Since the site is at the highest point eastwards until the Ural Mountains some 2,300 miles away, 842 miles east of Moscow, at least the missiles will have a low-level clear run...

RELIGION

At my time at school the morning assembly from infant through to secondary school involved a quasi-church service which included the Lord's Prayer, a hymn and a reading from the Bible. There was no choice whether to attend or not, other than a few Jewish kids who kept out of the way until the head teacher gave out notices or more often than not ticked us off for some misdemeanour that occurred on the previous day. That doesn't happen generally today in state schools.

When I was about nine years old, I was persuaded to join the Cubs which met in the Scout Hut next to St. Mary's Church in The Walk (now a car park).

Simply put, I just didn't get it. This entire dib-dib-dib lark and promising to do my best was bad enough but membership was conditional on going to the adjacent church every Sunday. Before I knew what was happening, I was forced to put on a cassock and found myself swinging incense in front of a sort of procession. It was all rather bewildering, alien and very different from the time I spent at Thomas a Becket Church Sunday School in Northaw a year or so earlier. My attendance didn't last long and I quietly faded away - no one seemed to notice.

St Mary's Church in the walk was built of 'Ranger's Patent Stone', a genteel term for concrete blocks, to replace the Church of St John the Baptist (on the present site of the War Memorial in the High Street). This was a plain, whitewashed, rectangular-shaped building, with a flat ceiling and plain glass. An enormous iron stove in the middle provided the  heating. In January 1911, a faulty gas lamp set fire to the roof with the net result that for some months the building was closed and services held in the Village Hall. The church, although then only a mere 75 years old, was doomed since apart from the damage it was considered too small and no great shakes architecturally anyway; it was decaying badly and incapable of expansion, thus it was considered necessary to build a new church.

The diocese granted £2,000 and by 1913 about £4,700 had been raised locally to replace it in The Walk. On 12 June 1915, the new Church of St Mary the Virgin and All Saints was consecrated. The Church Hall was built at the same time as the Church at a cost of around £2,000. But money ran out and faced with insurmountable debt and the ramifications of the First World War which was at its gruesome peak at that time, it was decided to leave St Mary's unfinished. It remained so for some years; I remember the curtain of corrugated iron covering the west wing. If you look carefully, you can just make out the join when it was eventually completed years later. It is such a shame that such a magnificent building and place of worship is hidden away in a minor road.

With apologies to the other denominations in the town, the other Anglican church is Charles the Martyr in Mutton Lane. Quite why it was named after Charles I (1625-1649) is somewhat baffling (there are three other similarly named churches in England: Falmouth, Peak District, Derbyshire and Tunbridge Wells). After all, he believed in the divine right of kings and didn't accept parliament's right to legislate, indeed he ruled without parliament for 11 years but then ran out of money and recalled it. The relationship was beyond saving. A bloody civil war began in 1642 and it is estimated that 200,000 English soldiers and civilians were killed by fighting and the diseases spread by armies - the loss was proportionate, population wise to that of World War 1. It is well known that Charles was ultimately defeated by the parliament army led by Oliver Cromwell in what was effectively a coup. Charles was found guilty of treason and beheaded on 30 January 1649. Not a great record to warrant being considered a martyr, I would suggest.

To this day I still have a somewhat jaundiced view of the High Church of England's pomp and circumstance. I've yet to be convinced that Jesus didn't exist and equally sure that the son of a carpenter may have felt as uncomfortable as me in such surroundings. Don't get me wrong - I support the whole ethos of Christianity: it's just the whole flummery that left me cold as a child which all these years later has never been revised. In short

I became a lukewarm socialist and a high church atheist which has remained with me.

According to a recent survey the UK is among the least religious countries in the world. In a global ranking of 65 countries, the UK came six places from last, with 30% of the population calling themselves religious. Far cleverer men than I have argued vociferously that the line of reasoning of our very existence is an amazing chance of nature and is admittedly persuasive. But for my part I find it difficult to identify with that hypothesis and remain quite content to go along with the Great Architect of the Universe until such time as someone convinces me otherwise. As a goldfish asked his companion in an aquarium whether he believed in God the reply he received was simple: 'Well, someone changes the water!'

What may be of interest is that when the German crew were killed as a result of the Zeppelin being shot down on 16 October 1916 and buried in the local cemetery in Mutton Lane, their graves were largely neglected until Hitler came to power in the 1930s and instituted 'Heroes Day' on 16 March 1935, to laud the soldiers of the past. Thus, annually on Armistice Day in November, a party from the German high command which occasionally included Hermann Goering, Rippentrop, Admiral Raeder, Propaganda Minister Goebbels et al would visit St Mary's so they could pay homage to the dead crew. After the service a fleet of Mercedes Benz limousines with swastikas fluttering would go on to the grave in Mutton Lane. A choir joined the German officials and relatives of the dead crew members. It was conducted entirely in German, involved Nazi salutes, swastikas and no doubt clicking heals. Nazi ambassador Joachim von Ribbentrop attended the ceremony in 1939 - a few months before the start of the Second World War. It is extraordinary to think that Nazi ceremonies were held annually in Potters Bar along with a retinue of black Mercedes cars sweeping through the town with swastikas fluttering proudly from the front bumpers. I can't imagine it went down well with the locals!

ROTTEN BOROUGH

With apologies to 'Private Eye'

It is perfectly understandable when old folk reminisce about their days of yore being so much better, particularly when they try to picture their environment in their early days. The town they lived in was much nicer, less noisy, less frantic and rosier. The neighbourhood wasn't scarred by modern buildings and the roads were less busy. Everything was, well, better and quieter - more on a human scale.

Changes are inevitable of course - it's called progress after all. It is natural to look back through rose-coloured spectacles at one's environment and neighbourhood and I make no apology for that. Out of all the towns of similar size in the UK, I would put Potters Bar's development at the top of the tree called calamitous. From the mid fifties the town has undergone unprecedented changes with buildings and spaces effectively owned by the local population who lived there being flogged off to the benefit of well, who? Not to the local population that's for sure.

Let me take you on an imaginary tour of what has happened since the fifties. For convenience I shall start at the bus station sans its wide green area in front of the depot - now a car park - and move along the High Street. Oakmere House, set on the edge of the park, which housed a ballroom and meeting rooms for the use of the general public, a small library and later a cinema-come-theatre - sold by the council to become a restaurant.

The frontage to Parkfield Park is opposite to Oakmere House. There was a delightful swage of pleasant greenery fronting Parkfield and its Japanese garden which was flogged off for housing. It was used twice a year to house a fair with hoopla stalls and dodgems taken away. We now have two lumps of flats that offend the eye with absolutely no architectural merit whatsoever, clearly influenced by the East German school of architecture and which would lie comfortably with giant Lego bricks.

Further up, opposite The Walk, is Salisbury House. And here's the rub, where did this money go? .... certainly not to the benefit of the beleaguered population. It had been used for meetings along with doctors' and dentists' surgeries and, yes, you've guessed, it was sold off by the council to a commercial developer.

Still further along the High Street what was Ladbroke School grounds are now scarred by flats, but the biggest disaster was the land owned by a Mr Tilbury that extended from the corner of the High Street running along the north side of Mutton Lane. As I understand it, he gave this for the benefit of the local populace. A hospital was built on part of the land (having moved from Richmond Road) and financed by public subscription. Well-designed, set back from the road, with deep greenery, it had a well-balanced frontage and was designed to be extended at a later date upwards in anticipation of future demands. It was taken over eventually with the formation of the National Health Service and the whole flogged off to a major supermarket which was more than happy to build a 'cottage hospital' squeezed into an inadequate piece of land in Barnet Road as part of the worse deal imaginable for the residents. A bad transaction all round, but this was insignificant when compared with the remainder of the land.

First the land between the original hospital and the Fire station was flogged off (I seem to use this expression with monotonous regularity) to a developer for housing was bad enough, but nothing compared with the rest of the land on the other side of the hospital towards the high street. It was sold to a developer for an office block to house the Gas Board (now the supermarket car park) - the remainder sold to Canada Life. We are now subjected to a huge mausoleum of a building set on the highest point of the town. When I say this offends the eye, there can be no argument. I was once told that this prime piece of land was sold on 28th April 1961 for £134,500 by the council which doesn't sound right to me either way... It's now worth - freehold - along with the monstrosity, many hundreds of millions of pounds. Not a bad deal for Canada Life and to a lesser extent British Gas, but what about the people of Potters Bar who lost out?

At the other end of town there were Council Offices near Potters Bar United Reformed Church which were sold for development as a couple detached houses along with the depot land at the corner of Mutton Lane and The Drive which was sold for redevelopment as flats - KERCHING! The moral of the story? If you own something that you would like benefit the town you live in after your demise, for Gawd's sake don't hand it over to the Council!

This is all rather disheartening to say the least, but one of the worst decisions made by the newly formed Council was the treatment of Wyllyotts Manor, the oldest building in the town. There was a delightful garden and lawn fronting what is now 'The Manor' pub and restaurant. It even had separate public toilets! This was a sort of de facto hub of the town – an opportunity to create a bit of greenery was chucked out of the window by building offices, car parking and probably the worse-designed 'Wyllyotts Centre', thrown up on the cheap. The exterior of this building is bad enough, but the inside is as welcoming as a small arms factory. The only greenery in Darkes Lane is the weeds growing between the broken paving slabs ... another opportunity lost. So, who is to blame for the flogging off of the family jewels? Other than central government edicts, responsibility must be laid at the doors of our elected Councillors. Whoever they were, they should be ashamed. And here's the rub, where did this money go? .... certainly not to the benefit of the beleaguered population.

It was April Fool's Day in 1974 that Potters Bar died.

Subject to the reorganisation of local government, the town was amalgamated with Borehamwood and other minor neighbourhoods. Potters Bar Urban District Council was no more. But why Borehamwood? With no direct public road or rail transport links it didn't make a lot of logistic sense.

Although 'mere' is in the title, the Oxford dictionary describes this as a lake or marsh and, yes, you guessed it, no such waterway exists either. So, who on earth came up with the brilliant suggestion of tying up with Borehamwood? Who came up with amalgamating with a remote town with no direct access?

The local consensus prior to its creation was that if it had to be done, then the direction north towards Hatfield and Welwyn Garden City was, in the words of Basil Fawlty, the bleeding obvious. Wouldn't it have been more sensible to tie up with the established and ancient connection routes? At least there is a straight, unhindered road, and train links. I can't remember this even being discussed. I fear that the civil service acted on a brief that was clothed with political reasons rather than pragmatic sense. All administration in the town simply disappeared. The entire population of Potters Bar henceforth had no direct physical access to Council offices. For a town of more than 22,000, the population was short-changed in spades. A huge expensive civic centre was built in Elstree Way, Borehamwood whilst, for a short time, a cramped little office was squeezed into Wyllyotts Manor that opened between 10am and 4pm twice a week and had one receptionist. After a while even that closed. Face-to-face consultation? Forget it!

Potters Bar has always been on the edge of things geographically. The writer came across an old AA pre-War book listing not only road routes, but also a brief description of towns. When I looked up Potters Bar it simply said 'See South Mimms'. An up-to-date description might now be 'See Borehamwood'.

The town was originally in Middlesex on the northern edge of the county - effectively a peninsular that ran through southwards, as far as Twickenham. Consequently, the constabulary was the Metropolitan Police which remained for a while after the town was transferred into Hertfordshire. The old police station at the top of Coopers Lane - sadly flogged off to be now used as a nursery - still has the sign to confirm its designation. Middlesex is no more after the reorganisation and the only remnant left is the County Cricket Club based at Lords.

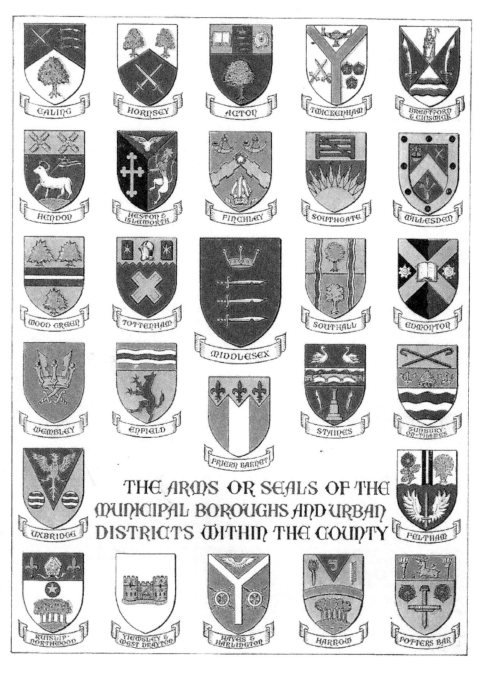

THE ARMS OR SEALS OF THE MUNICIPAL BOROUGHS AND URBAN DISTRICTS WITHIN THE COUNTY

Potters Bar is at the end unsurprisingly.

Now we are on the edge of the county of Hertfordshire instead, of course, this time at the southern end, which is on the edge of the capital, in a country which is on the edge of Europe, in a world which is on the edge of the Milky Way. Perhaps this peculiarity of location has in an odd way been its attraction. Being different.

A LA RECHERCHE DU TEMPS PERDU

Back in the days of tanners and bobs, when Mothers had patience and Fathers had jobs.

When football teams you played for wore hand-me-down shoes and TV had only two channels in order to choose.

Back in days of threepenny bits, when schools employed nurses to search for your nits.

When snowballs were harmless, ice slides were permitted and your jumpers were warm and hand knitted.

When cars were so rare you could play in the street, when doctors made house calls and police walked the beat.

It was dumplings for dinner and trifle for tea and your annual break was just a day by the sea.

When woodwork and pottery got taught in schools and everyone dreamed of a win on the pools.

Roller skates and trolley riding; snowballs to lob, back in days of tanners and bobs.

have gone through life accepting the 'ups and downs' and treating those two imposters just the same (sorry Rudyard), being outwardly genial (depending who I talked to) with bouts of melancholy in between when on my own. When some of my grumpy contemporaries go on about 'the good old days', compared with the 'bad old days' of today, I think of living in my days of youth and experiencing, for example, no central heating or fridge or a family motor car along with none of the labour-saving things we take for granted today.

All true, and yet, while I count all these blessings, I have a sort of creeping despair of late and my concern is aimed at the next generation. My grandchildren's world is facing global warming, pollution, food shortages, bullies from the east, AI threat and not being able to buy their own house. The one elephant in the room is the number of migrants to this already crowded country which has exceeded seven million in the last twenty years and shows no sign of slowing down, a population which has more than doubled in my lifetime. I could go on.....

I think of the amazing advances in medicine. From my middle age I have suffered from rheumatoid arthritis and when eventually diagnosed, no prescribed medication simply didn't work. At night and first thing in the morning I could hardly move and when I did it was damned painful. I had to give up squash and golf which was a great wrench - particularly the social drink with my mates afterwards. Using a wheelchair was a chore.

My rheumatologist having tried various medications over a couple of years eventually came up with Enbrel. He had to obtain the 'thumbs-up' from NICE because it is expensive. I inject it once a week. I can now get around OK if a bit creakily (but that goes with the ageing process after all). Thank God for the NHS and research chemists, I say. It is wonderful having a free national health service for all its faults and despite its lack of investment which my parents never had through a significant period of their lives. As for university education, almost 50% now go to university compared with 4% in my day. That must be an advance even if it has to be paid for. There is a lot of moaning and pessimism around from my generation. But it is fire which is fanned by the media. People believe there are more burglaries and violent crimes than there were, more deaths in 'plane crashes or on the roads – all nonsense. Wall-to-wall news coverage is always bad, it seems. Good news is only covered by advertisements.

I am far better off financially than my parents were. I jointly own a fully paid-for house, which other than for a brief period they never did. The 'bank of Mum and Dad' is based mainly on my lucky generation living at a period in housing history when you even got a tax rebate on your mortgage. We are overall a much more tolerant society. Homosexuality was against the law in the sixties. Single mothers were ostracised, forced to give away their babies. We are a diverse, ethnically mixed society and in the main we all get on OK. We have not been in a world war for almost eighty years. We care about the climate and want to undo the damage we have done.

All true, and yet, while I count all these blessings, I have a sort of creeping despair of late and my concern is aimed at the next generation. My grandchildren's world: global warming, pollution, the population explosion (in this Country it has doubled in my lifetime), mass immigration from poor countries, food, bullies from the east. I could go on.

Of course, I get angry on occasions - it goes with the territory. Listening to a recorded message on the telephone saying that my call is important when it clearly isn't, otherwise they would answer the bloody thing. Not being able to see a doctor face-to-face when there is something wrong. Waiting hours in A&E. Speeding cars, cyclists on the pavement, those kids on motorized scooters. Cooking and stupid quiz programs on TV along with anything that has 'celebrity' in the title. Politicians and the House of Commons, local councillors, people and companies that don't pay their fair share in tax. Finally, bloody computers, junk mail and mobile phones that allegedly have been programmed to make life easier but do quite the opposite at precisely the wrong time.

So, the clarion call? Perhaps just to take time to smell the flowers, take a sip of wine, count your blessings, keep calm, and carry on....

WHAT POTTERS BAR IS FAMOUS FOR?

What Potters Bar is famous for (other than the M25):

1. 'Bloodbath at the House of Death' film released in 1984 featuring, amongst others, Vincent Price - the only occasion he starred as a comedy actor.
2. 'Digby, The Biggest Dog in the World' -released in 1973: circus tent erected in a field opposite 204 -210 Barnet Road; internal shots in a house opposite 'The White Hart' in South Mymms.
3. Two murders at Potters Bar Golf Club, one of them infamous as 'The Murder of the Seventeenth Tee' in the late fifties.
4. Train crash on10 May 2002 resulting in seven deaths.

Famous people who lived in Potters Bar:

1. Tony Jacklin, golfer, assistant professional at Potters Bar Golf Club, winner of both the Open at Royal Lytham St Annes and the U.S. Open at Hazeltine. Ryder Cup captain from 1983-89.
2. Acker Bilk, clarinetist.
3. Terry Lightfoot, traditional jazz player.
4. Johnnie Wright, the 1948 Amateur Boxing Association British middleweight title holder, Silver medalist in the 1948 London Olympics.
5. Glenn Taylor (my son) who was Captain of the England Rugby Union Colts XV.

ACKNOWLEDGMENTS

The Story of Potters Bar & South Mimms Published in 1966

The Dogs by Laura Thompson

Modernity Britain by David Kynaston

The Rock N' Roll Age by Mike Evans

Mount Grace Journals

Oakmere Public Library

Ready Steady Go! By Chris Tarrant

Northaw and Cuffley by Millington & Higgs

Hertfordshire Curiosities by John Lucas

History of the Ritz by Molly Drinnan

InterPro Publishing Solutions - Mark Gedye

Printed in Great Britain
by Amazon

23490611R00069